Dr. Dominik Reither, M.A.

A German Prisoner of War Camp 1939-1945

Stalag VII A
Moosburg

Bibliografische Information der Deutschen Nationalbibliothek:
Die Deutsche Nationalbibliothek verzeichnet diese Publikation in der Deutschen
Nationalbibliografie; detaillierte bibliografische Daten sind im Internet über dnb.dnb.de
abrufbar.

Bibliographic information of the German National Library:
The German National Library lists this publication in the German National Bibliography;
detailed bibliographic data are available on the Internet at dnb.dnb.de.

1st English edition 2023
Translation of the German edition 2015

© Dr. Dominik Reither 2015

ISBN 9783757861605

Author: Dr. Dominik Reither, M.A.

Editor: Stalag Moosburg e.V.

Production and publishing: BoD – Books on Demand, Norderstedt, Germany

Photos: Private Archive Karl A. Bauer
Municipal Archives Moosburg

Translation: DeepL.com
Proofreading: Karen Carlson, Marilyn Walton

Layout and prepress: Günther Strehle

Dr. Dominik Reither

Stalag VII A Moosburg – A Prisoner of War Camp 1939 – 1945

Translation of the German edition 2015

Table of Contents

Greeting from Mrs Anita Meinelt

April 1945 meant not only the end of the war for Moosburg, but also the liberation of the prisoner of war camp Stalag VII A. The camp is an essential part of the town's history, which until now has hardly been the focus of public interest. It is time to deal with this topic, because after decades of neglect, today's generation perceives its history in an unbiased and curious way. Former opponents have become partners and friends. Integration is a topical political and social issue. Understanding history can help us to become aware of the fragility of these relationships.

Our history is part of the identity of our city, which distinguishes us from other cities. We experience supra-regional and international interest with it. I, therefore, see it as a task of the city to support research and documentation about Stalag VII A. My special thanks go to Dr. Dominik Reither, whose work offers us a valuable contribution to this endeavor.

Anita Meinelt

Mayor of the City of Moosburg a. d. Isar

Moosburg, 2015

Greeting from Mr Herbert Franz

Remembering the past is one thing. To work through the past historically and to get to know it is another thing. Over the past decades, many people in Moosburg have volunteered to collect and archive information about this period of Moosburg's history. They deserve our thanks for their dedication. Many items, writings, reports, photographs, newspaper accounts, eyewitness testimony, even various works of art exist from this period, collected in private hands, the local history museum, on internet sites, and in the Municipal Archives. Many things are subjectively reported; they are individual pieces of a mosaic, which only when put together form a picture. The Stalag Moosburg e.V. association has made it a priority to bring this information together and, thus, make it more accessible.

An essential step in this direction is now the research of Dr. Dominik Reither. For the first time after 70 years, there is now a scientifically-sound account that can serve as a recognized basis for further research and investigation.

I would like to thank Dr. Dominik Reither for his dedicated voluntary professional work. I hope that this brochure generates much interest and attention.

Herbert Franz

Chairman Stalag Moosburg e.V.

Moosburg, 2015

Foreword

A preface is the place to thank all those who contributed to the creation of this brochure: the association Stalag Moosburg e.V. with Herbert Franz, who sparked interest in the history of Stalag VII A and Günther Strehle, who coordinated the layout and financing as part of the "70 Years of Liberation" project; Karl A. Bauer, who provided the pictures from his extensive online archive; the staff of the Regensburg University Library, the Moosburg City Library, the Munich State Archives, and especially the Moosburg City Archives, for its continual support in the research. I would also like to thank my wife, Christine Metterlein-Reither, who critically commented and meticulously proofread the individual chapters. Special thanks go to the City of Moosburg for bearing the production costs.

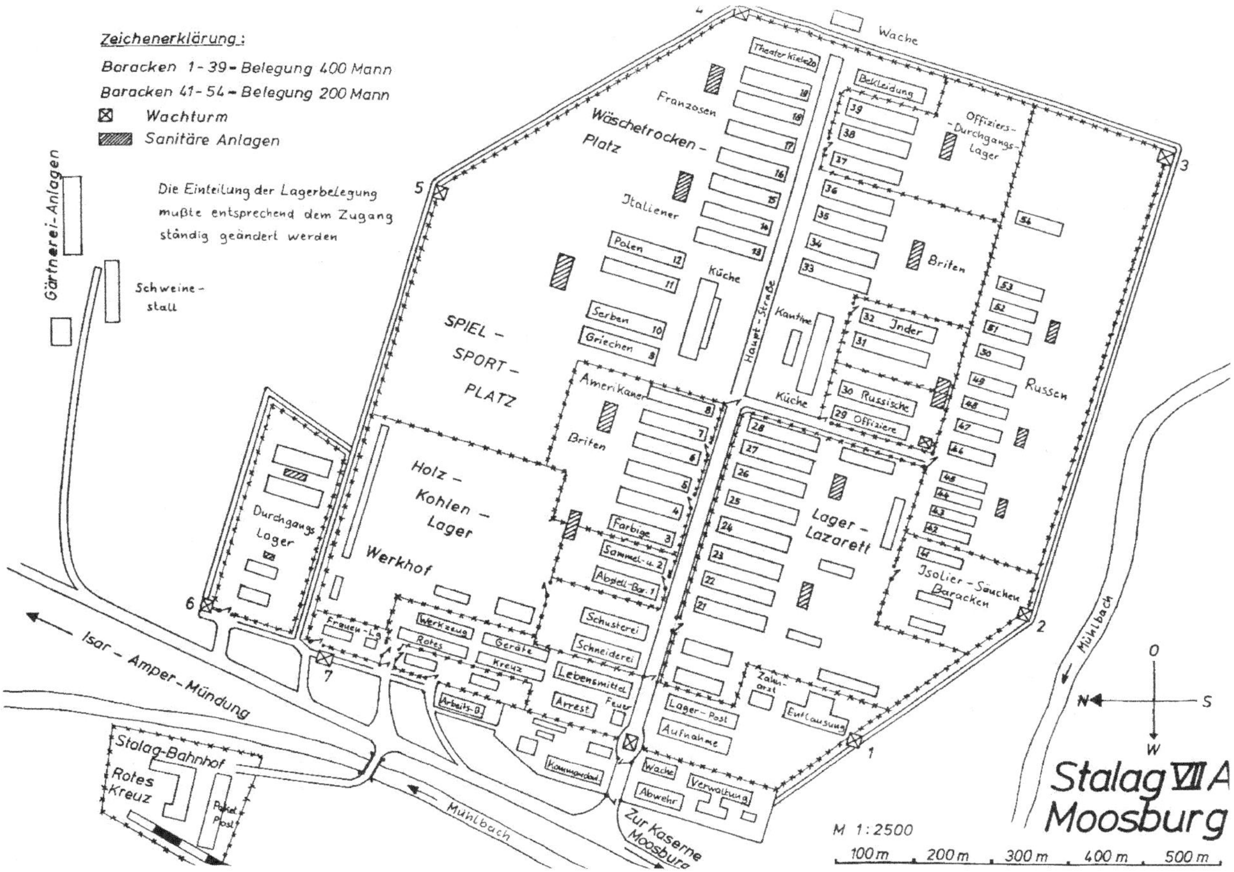

Figure 1: Stalag VII A Camp plan

Legend:

Barracks 1-39 allocation 400 men
Barracks 41-54 allocation 200 men

⊠   Watchtower
▭   Sanitary facilities

The arrangement of the camp allocation had to be
constantly changed according to the arrival of POW

Durchgangslager	Transit camp
Werkhof	Workshop
Holz-Kohlen-Lager	Wood and Coal Storage
Spiel-Sport-Platz	Play and Sports Field
Wäschetrockenplatz	Laundry drying place
Lager-Lazarett	Camp hospital
Aufnahme	Reception and registration

1. Introduction

Seventy years after the end of World War II and the collapse of the Third Reich, the period of National Socialism is one of the best-researched periods of German history. But still there are some areas that historians, so far, have not paid much attention. The prisoner of war (POW) system of the German Wehrmacht and the life of prisoners of war in the camps are among them. This is due in part to the fact that the sources are extremely scarce. Extensive files of the Wehrmacht were destroyed at the end of the war or have disappeared. For example, the names of all the commandants of many camps are not even known. In contrast, the source material for the POW base camp (Mannschaftsstammlager) Stalag VII A Moosburg is comparatively good. In addition to the files of military offices, the Moosburg Municipal Archives have also preserved large collections on many aspects of the prisoner-of-war system.

This brochure deals with various issues related to Stalag VII A, such as the construction and liberation of the camp, the care of prisoners, work assignments and leisure time, or prisoners' contact with the general population. The individual chapters do not claim to be exhaustive. Not all aspects can be addressed, and some areas can only be dealt with as an overview. Neither the material in the various archives, nor the secondary literature could be evaluated and considered in their entirety.

2. Choice of Moosburg as location for a prisoner of war camp

"But in 14 days a camp for 10,000 prisoners of war has to be here," Colonel Nepf, the first commandant of the Moosburg POW camp, is quoted as saying in the transcript of a lecture he gave in January 1941.[1]

Why was Moosburg chosen as the site of a prison camp, and why was the construction so hasty?

Many of the files of the departments involved have been lost, but the events can still be reconstructed relatively well.

Decision-makers and structures

In simplified terms, the decision-making structures in the fall of 1939 were as follows: The highest authority with regard to prisoners of war was the Wehrmacht General Command (Oberkommando der Wehrmacht "OKW"). It was there that the basic decisions were made. At the intermediate level, the commands of a military district were responsible for regulating the detailed issues of the so-called prisoner of war (POW) system and for organizing the camps in their area. The commands of a military district were the central command offices of the Wehrmacht at the level of the military districts. The entire Reich territory was divided into such military districts. Moosburg was located in military district VII (Munich), which comprised the southern half of Bavaria from the Alps to the Danube (northern Bavaria formed military district XIII).[2]

The individual camps were numbered according to the military districts with Roman numerals, and then the camps within a military district were designated with letters according to the alphabet, in the order in which they were set up. In military district VII there were two POW camps, Stalag VII A Moosburg and Stalag VII B Memmingen. The abbreviation "Stalag" stands for "Mannschaftsstammlager" (base camp) for non-commissioned officers and enlisted men. There were also several Oflags (officers' camps) in the military district VII area, including one in Murnau.[3]

Principles for the siting of a POW camp

Initially, the mobilization orders of the Wehrmacht in the fall of 1939 designated the northern and eastern military districts, predominantly in the agricultural regions of the Reich such as East Prussia or Brandenburg, for the reception of Polish prisoners. The background to this was that the OKW wanted to use the prisoners for work in agriculture in order to compensate for the loss of German labor due to conscription into the Wehrmacht. Probably because the number of captured Polish soldiers was much larger than expected, the OKW had prison camps set up in other military districts from September 1939 onwards. Therefore, in mid-September 1939, the OKW requested the command of military district VII to determine a location for the construction of a POW camp in the Landshut area. The exact determination was left to the command of the military district. One reason for the choice of a location "near Landshut" could be that this region was relatively central in the military district and close to a main railway line. The prisoners could, therefore, be easily transported by train to the camp and from there to work assignments throughout the military district, especially in the agricultural areas of Lower Bavaria.[4]

Why Moosburg, in particular, was chosen, however, can be deduced to a certain extent from Army Regulation 38/12 "Service Instructions on Space Requirements, Construction and Furnishing of a Prisoner-of-War Camp". According to these instructions, the supply of water was the primary criterion in the selection of a site. Further criteria were a remote, but nevertheless convenient, location, the supply of electricity, and a hygienically-safe disposal of sewage. The plots should be regularly limited, clear and protected, but agriculturally inferior.[5]

Colonel Nepf was not enthusiastic about the Moosburg site. In his opinion, "from the point of view of the landscape and hygiene ... the choice of site for the establishment of a camp was hardly to be advocated, but one had 'other sound reasons'".[6] However, he does not mention these. The negative assessment of the camp commander could also have been made because he wanted to highlight his achievement and that of his people, namely the construction of a large camp in a short time despite numerous adverse circumstances. The report quoted above is written in a similar tone. The site, however, despite Colonel Nepf's negative assessment, met most of the requirements of Army Regulation 38/12. Irrigation and drainage could be provided at Moosburg. The site was in close proximity to a central railroad line, but was still relatively far from major public roads. It was also secluded due to rivers, woods, and floodplains; moreover, the area of the future camp was at some distance from the city. Land and soil were of rather poor quality agriculturally.

The decision for Moosburg

The records of the then-mayor, Müller, show that the decision to build the Stalag in Moosburg was made within a few days. On September 19, 1939, less than three weeks after the beginning of the war, Mayor Müller noted that on the same day two gentlemen from the Munich local planning office had visited him and informed him that the Munich army administration was looking for a suitable site for a prison camp. An area in the Untere Gereuth between Mühlbach and the city/state forest had been inspected, which seemed suitable because it was far from public roads and had sufficient cover by forest and trees. Thus, it fulfilled the requirements of the above-mentioned army service regulations. Apparently, Mayor Müller was left largely in the dark as he wrote that details would be known in the coming days. After further inspections by Wehrmacht officers, the command of military district determined Moosburg as the camp site after only a few days, according to Mayor Müller's notes on September 21, and according to Wehrmacht records on September 22.[7]

Figure 2 Location of the Stalag complex in the city territory of Moosburg (1) Barracks of the guards, (2) Prisoners of war camp

Many prisoners as the reason for the rush

Those responsible in the Wehrmacht were probably surprised by the large number of Polish soldiers taken prisoner within just a few days. Estimates of how many Polish soldiers fell into German captivity vary widely. German reports from 1939 speak of approximately 700,000 prisoners. This figure was also adopted by some of the research community. Other historians assume about 540,000 prisoners, some Polish historians about 440,000.[8] These soldiers were captured in the few weeks between September 1 and October 6, the surrender of the last Polish troops. In a very short time, the Wehrmacht had to supply and house a large number of prisoners. In purely mathematical terms, given the standard size of 10,000 prisoners per camp originally planned by the Wehrmacht, between 44 and 70 camps were needed to accommodate the Polish soldiers.[9] The excessive number of prisoners not only led to the fact that camps were now also set up in military districts which had not initially been selected for this purpose. Building of these unplanned camps also, had to be done in a great hurry.

The following order shows that the Wehrmacht was overwhelmed by the large number of prisoners: On September 21, 1939, the OKW called upon the military districts to expand the camps to full occupancy as quickly as possible and to make "ruthless" use of suitable public and private grounds. A temporary cramped occupancy with prisoners had to be accepted.[10]

3. Construction of Stalag VII A

Structure of a POW camp

Army regulation 38/12 precisely regulated the structure and equipment of a prisoner-of-war camp. According to this model regulation for a "standard camp," the guard and office barracks were located at the entrance. This was followed by the ante-camp with the so-called functional barracks for reception/registration, disinfection, fuel, medical care and workshops. In this part of the camp, newly arriving prisoners were searched, registered, deloused, and given an identification badge before being housed in the living quarters of the main camp. The main camp, which according to the Wehrmacht's conception was supposed to hold 10,000 prisoners, was divided into ten groups. Each group consisted of four accommodation barracks for 250 prisoners each and one abort barrack. The individual groups were separated from each other by barbed wire. Two kitchen barracks and one store barrack were to be built approximately in the middle of the camp. The construction and size of the barracks were specified in detail. For each prisoner, 2.5 square meters, and for each guard, 3 square meters of space, were estimated. A double barbed wire fence ran around the camp.[11]

Army Regulation 38/12 also prescribed a precise schedule for the construction of the camp. After 90 days, the living barracks, the light, irrigation and drainage systems, as well as the roads, were to be built; after 120 days, the camp had to be completely finished.[12]

However, commanders were advised in Army Regulation 38/5 that camps had to accept prisoners from day one. Only a wire fence was necessary for a camp to go into operation. The fact that initially, these camps could only be provisional facilities, was accepted by those in charge of the Wehrmacht. In the early days, the prisoners were to be housed in tents and makeshift huts, which they were then to convert into permanent barracks themselves.[13]

Construction of the Moosburg POW camp

In the first months, much of Stalag VII A Moosburg, was only provisional, too. On September 22, 1939, Colonel Nepf, the first camp commander, and several doctors entered the area north of the town for the first time, which had been designated by General Command VII as the location for a prisoner-of-war camp. At that time, the area was still mostly arable land, gravel, soil, and loam, and the fields were still cultivated with cabbage, turnips and potatoes. A swamp stretched out towards the Isar, behind it came woods and meadows. There was only a fertilizer factory, a mill and sheds. These were intended as emergency shelters, among other things. According to instructions from the command of military district, Colonel Nepf and his staff had to set up a camp for 10,000 prisoners within 14 days.[14]

Figure 3: Construction of housing barracks

At the end of September, the Reich Labor Service began building the camp. The Reich Labor Service was mandated to build the camp in ten days.[15] Considering the detailed construction specifications of the Army Service Regulations, for which the Wehrmacht had estimated a construction time of 120 days, the two aforementioned deadlines could not mean that the camp was to be completely built, but that within 10 and 14 days, respectively, the camp was to be ready to receive prisoners.

The Command of Military District considered the construction of a delousing facility to be particularly important, since the General Command of the Wehrmacht had announced "non-decontaminated" prisoners in poor clothing.[16] This was that due to the often chaotic conditions at the front and the poor hygienic conditions in the prisoner assembly centers and transit camps; lice was widespread. The diseases they transmitted posed a real danger of epidemics given the close occupancy of the camps. For this reason, great importance was attached to delousing the prisoners.[17]

The Reich Labor Service, therefore, erected a makeshift delousing station in a hall of an artificial fertilizer factory. The "delousing station" was comprised of a facility with 16 showers and was completed on October 4, 1939. It was presented as a model at a meeting of camp doctors in Berlin in February 1940. However, it was still only a provisional procedure in the autumn of 1940. Heating for the delousing station was provided by the heating car of a hospital train, later by two old locomotives.[18]

While the cooking had initially been done outdoor, the Reich Labor Service later erected the kitchen facility. This was 80-by-4 meters in size. Posts were driven into the soft ground as foundations. In mid-October 1939, 25 tents were erected as the first accommodation for the prisoners. Each could accommodate about 200 men.[19]

Bad weather, especially rain, hampered the construction work from the beginning of October. The mud was half-a-meter deep in places. With these conditions, the camp received its first prisoners on October 19.[20]

The make-shift condition of Stalag VII A (Moosburg) was not an isolated case. In Stalag II D (Stargard/Pomerania), Polish prisoners had to sleep in tents without straw or blankets until 1940. Other military districts also improvised, accommodating prisoners in factories or barracks: Stalag VI A (Hemer) was located in former barracks, VI D (Dortmund) in the Dortmund Westfalenhalle.[21]

Problems with the procurement of building materials

So, on September 22, 1939, the first materials for the construction of the camp were ordered, among others 100 km of barbed wire and 70 tents of 420 square meters each for 150 men.[22] Colonel Nepf indicated that it was quite problematic to obtain building materials and supplies for the operation of the camp. For example, he praised the organizational skills of the head of the Reich Labor Service Unit, who procured iron, cement, bricks, and wood for the construction of the delousing station "without a code number," i.e., outside the official allotment. Colonel Nepf's statements show how chaotic the conditions were in the procurement of materials. "Self-help was the trump card, with us and with others...Steal, rob, murder and do not get caught .... So .... we too acted after some hesitation. If we had not done so, the camp would still be only fields, meadows, swamps and forests today." Although these statements are obviously exaggerated in order to keep the audience of the lecture engaged, two examples used by Colonel Nepf show that even at the beginning of the war, material was embezzled on a large scale, sometimes even within the Wehrmacht. He spoke of front-line troops "stealing" (!) 16,000 square meters of roofing that he felt were destined for Stalag VII A. He also indicated that a railway accident in a small town in Württemberg was faked in order to divert 90 tons of coal destined for Stalag VII A, which resulted in insufficient heating in the camp.[23]

Need for land

Part of the camp was built on agricultural land. About 200,000 square meters of fields were needed. Those responsible for building the camp showed little consideration for the landowners, who had to cede their land.[24] The city tried to provide compensation for the farmers, but this was only partially successful.[25] The landowners were immediately notified against signature to clear their fields "without delay".[26] This did not work in every case. The Reich Labor Service was not always able to erect tents as shelters for the prisoners as

Figure 4: Photo from the early days of the camp: In the foreground an already completed housing barrack, in the background tents as preliminary accommodation.

planned in mid-October, because beets and potatoes had not yet been completely harvested.[27]

Size of the camp site

Colonel Nepf also reported on the size of the camp (as of January 1941). It extended over an area of 600-by-550 meters. The main road of the camp had a length of 670 meters; in total, the crossroads came to 7,250 meters. The enclosed space of all accommodations, including the commandant's and guard barracks, amounted to 171,000 cubic meters.[28]

4. Arrival of the first prisoners of war in Stalag VII A on Oct. 19, 1939

Organization of a POW camp

For the management, administration and operation of a "standard camp" with 10,000 prisoners, 98 soldiers (14 officers, 23 non-commissioned officers and 61 enlisted men) as well as 33 military officials and employees were planned for, according to the Wehrmacht personnel key.[29] According to Army Regulation 38/5, these personnel were divided into six so-called "groups," namely the groups "Commandant," "Labor Deployment," "Medical Officer," "Counterintelligence and Postal Surveillance," "Administration," and "Motor Pool." The counterintelligence officer, the head of the "Counterintelligence and Postal Surveillance" group, had particularly-extensive powers. In addition to checking letters and parcels, he was responsible for countering sabotage and espionage, for interrogating prisoners, and for securing the camp. The counterintelligence officer was instructed to maintain close contact with the Gestapo in order to perform his duties.[30]

The camp commandant and his deputy were appointed by the General Command of the Wehrmacht. In most Stalags, they were older military personnel who were no longer fit for front-line duty.[31] In Moosburg, at least in the beginning, some of the Stalag personnel had private quarters in the town.[32]

Landesschützen battalions were responsible for guarding the prisoners. Such a battalion consisted of three companies of four officers, 19 non-commissioned officers and 129 men as well as a staff company. The Landesschützen battalion 512 was assigned to Stalag VII A. The Landesschützen battalions were mostly recruited from older men or those only partially fit for war and were only lightly armed.[33] The quarters of the Landesschützen assigned to guard the camp were located in a complex of barracks south of the Stalag grounds. The battalion had a military hospital in what is now the Anton Vitzthum Elementary School.[34]

Arrival of the first prisoners

Immediately after capture in the combat zone in Poland, officers and enlisted men were separated and the soldiers were initially taken to prisoner assembly points near the front. These were makeshift camps in warehouses, barracks or sports fields. After a few days, the prisoners were taken from there to the transit camps (Dulag), either in Poland or in the eastern part of the Reich, where they were registered and housed until they could be distributed among the prison camps in the Reich. In the prisoner assembly centers and the Dulags, there was often insufficient food and supplies. In addition, poor hygienic conditions prevailed, so that lice often spread among the prisoners. Since they transmitted diseases, lice posed a considerable danger

Figure 5: A group of prisoners on the way to the camp

for the occurrence of epidemics due to the close occupancy of the camps.[35]

On October 19, 1939, i.e. already after the end of the fighting in Poland (October 6, 1939), the first 1400 prisoners arrived in Moosburg by train at about 6 p.m., according to Colonel Nepf, the first camp commandant. They were filthy, exhausted and hungry. Since it was raining heavily, the prisoners were fed soup and coffee while still on the train, which had been driven along an industrial track to the camp's delousing plant. There, they also spent the night. In order to prevent lice from being brought into the camp, the prisoners were not allowed to enter the camp grounds until they had been deloused. This procedure, which lasted 15 hours, began at 7 a.m. on October 20. Since the reception facilities had not yet been completed, only 500 prisoners could wait for delousing in a covered factory hall, protected from bad weather. The remaining 900 had to stay outside at first. In case of rain, later, the camp staff provided them with tents. The delousing facility was heated with an old heating car from a military hospital train, whose proclivity to failures led to delays.

On the German side, numerous interpreters and scribes were employed to register the prisoners. The camp administration attached great importance to thorough registration. In addition, the prisoners were searched as part of the registration procedure, and files, weapons, valuables and cash were taken from them, as well as all other dangerous objects or objects that could facilitate an escape, such as pocket knives, tools, flashlights or all substances that could be used to make secret ink.[36]

Figure 6: The first prisoners had to be accommodated in tents because the housing barracks were not yet completed; in the background the city of Moosburg

Since it was already relatively cold, and rainwater was flowing into some of the tents that were actually intended to accommodate the prisoners, the prisoners were housed on the first floor of a warehouse located on the grounds, contrary to regulations, since fire protection was not guaranteed.[37]

In the first months of the Stalag's existence, much was only makeshift. Since the barracks had not yet been completed, the prisoners had to sleep primarily in tents.

This was not unusual in German prison camps in the autumn/winter of 1939-1940.

This situation was extremely problematic for the prisoners in view of the bad weather in the autumn of 1939. It rained a lot, so that the groundwater rose and washed out the makeshift infirmary, mortar fell from the ceilings, water ran from the walls and the bedclothes became moldy. On December 7, 1939, wet snow came, tent walls burst, barbed wire fences collapsed, electrical cables broke and the latrines overflowed.[38]

Nevertheless, numerous prisoners were brought to Stalag VII A. On the cut-off date of Dec. 13, 1939 there were already 9,040 Polish prisoners in its area of responsibility.[39]

Planning for a work assignment of prisoners of war in Moosburg

The city administration of Moosburg was also preparing for the arrival of the prisoners. Mayor Müller thought about what projects the prisoners could be used for. The mayor thought of the municipal sewage system, the road to the village of Hörgersdorf, roads in "settlement areas" and a drainage system for the dairy. He immediately asked the local dairy to submit a drainage concept.[40]

As early as the late fall of 1939, POW from the camp were used by the city for road construction, and later, in larger numbers, for construction work enlarging the city's sewage system.[41]

5. Postal system

"Never give chocolate in whole bars, but only by fractions!" read the "Letter and Parcel Post" service instructions of Stalag VII A.[42] Prisoners of war could receive and send mail according to the regulations of the Geneva Convention. In everyday camp life, the postal system played an important role for the prisoners, but also for the camp administration, for various reasons.

Situation of the prisoners

In order to appreciate the importance of postal service for the prisoners, one must bear in mind their situation. After the admission procedure (delousing and registration), a prisoner found himself in the main part of the camp, housed in simple barracks in a confined space, without any privacy. At the same time, it was

Figure 7: A group of prisoners

completely unclear how long the imprisonment would last and what the future would hold. Despite all the rules of protection under international law, the prisoners were at the mercy of the German military. Last but not least, often for weeks, the prisoners had no opportunity to inform their families of their fate or to find out if their relatives had survived the turmoil of war. Prof. Dr. Ziegler, who cared for prisoners from Stalag VII A as a chaplain, also noted that in many Poles and French there was "dejection" due to the rapid defeats at the hands of the German troops. These circumstances had even led to psychological disorders, which could range from pessimism to fatalism and go as far as suicide.[43]

Postal service was, therefore, of enormous importance to the prisoners, as letters were the only way to maintain contact with home, with family, and in a certain sense, with the old life. In concrete terms, food parcels improved the supply situation, and books, tools, games or musical instruments sent by mail made it possible to expand leisure activities.[44]

Letter post

However, postal service was subject to various regulations. First, the number of letters and postcards that a prisoner could send was limited. The quotas varied according to nationality. French, Polish and Serbian prisoners were allowed to write two letters and two postcards per month. Italian military internees were allowed two letters and four postcards per month. Soviet prisoners were allowed to write one letter or card per month, but only to Reich territory, occupied territories, or neutral or allied foreign countries.[45] This means that there was no possibility for Soviet prisoners to keep in touch with their relatives in those parts of the Soviet Union, which were not occupied by German troops.

All correspondence with non-related persons in Germany, German members of the Wehrmacht or military services (with the exception of camp commandant's offices), with services of the home country and with legations, consulates and military attachés inside and outside Germany was forbidden.[46]

For letters and postcards there were forms that were printed bilingually, in German and the respective national language. There were also forms for the replies of the relatives. Mail was only forwarded if both prisoner and relatives used these forms and filled them out properly, namely in pencil on the pre-printed lines.[47]

Incoming and outgoing letters and postcards were subject to censorship in the camp. Within the camp administration, the "Counterintelligence Group" under the direction of the counterintelligence officer was responsible for postal matters and, above all, for censoring prisoner mail in the entire Stalag area. For this purpose, the prisoners' mail from the work detachments and the branch camps was brought to the censorship office of the Stalag. Interpreters were responsible for censorship. They had to proceed according to an inspector's primer, which gave instructions on how to detect secret inks or hidden messages. Before a mail item could be forwarded, it had to be stamped with a censor's stamp. Each censor had his own numbered censorship stamp, so that it could be traced who had checked a specific mail item and in this way the censors, in turn, could also be monitored. Among other things, prisoners were forbidden to state their whereabouts. The prisoners also had to refrain from making any anti-German statements in their letters, otherwise the letters would not be forwarded. Some prisoners tried to circumvent the censorship and forward their letters via German civilians. This, or even just giving stamps to prisoners, was strictly forbidden for both civilians and military personnel.[48]

Around 1940, 50 German officers, non-commissioned officers and enlisted men were employed in Stalag VII A to monitor the mail. In one month, 140,000 letters were received and 70,000 letters were sent. Near the entrance to the camp was the camp mail barracks. One hundred eighty prisoners assisted in handling postal matters.[49] Prisoners also handled the distribution of mail in the camp itself. Much of the mail traffic between the POW and their homelands went through the International Committee of the Red Cross (ICRC). Americans and British were even able to send their letters by airmail - upon payment of appropriate fees.[50]

Parcel post

Prisoners were also allowed to receive parcels. According to a leaflet issued by the General Command of the Wehrmacht in July 1942, prisoners of war could receive parcels from private individuals or from aid societies in neutral or enemy countries. For the British,

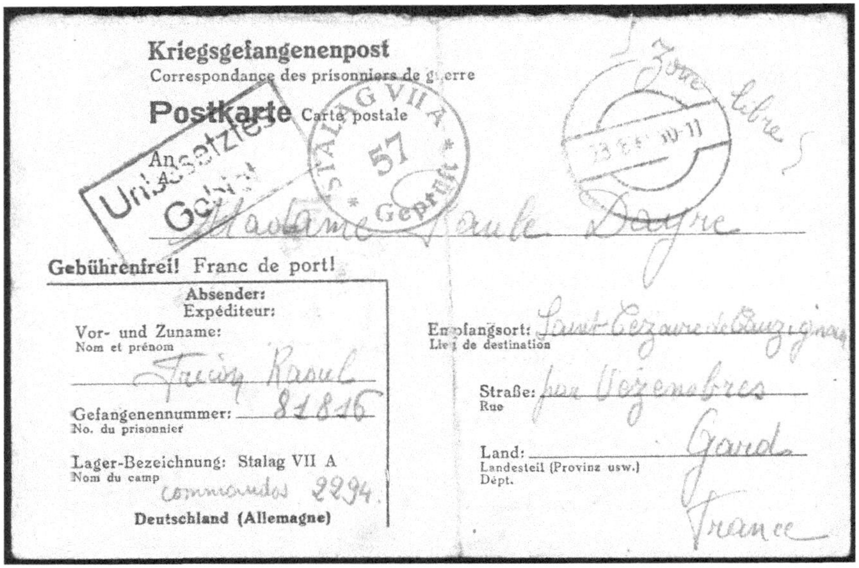
Kriegsgefangenenpost
Correspondance des prisonniers de guerre
Postkarte Carte postale
An / A: Madame Paule Dayre
Gebührenfrei! Franc de port!
Absender: / Expéditeur:
Vor- und Zuname: / Nom et prénom:
Gefangenennummer: / No. du prisonnier: 81816
Lager-Bezeichnung: Stalag VII A / Nom du camp: commandos 2294.
Deutschland (Allemagne)
Empfangsort: / Lieu de destination:
Straße: / Rue:
Land: / Landesteil (Provinz usw.) / Dépt.: Gard / France
Unbesetztes Gebiet
STALAG VII A 57 Geprüft
Zone libre

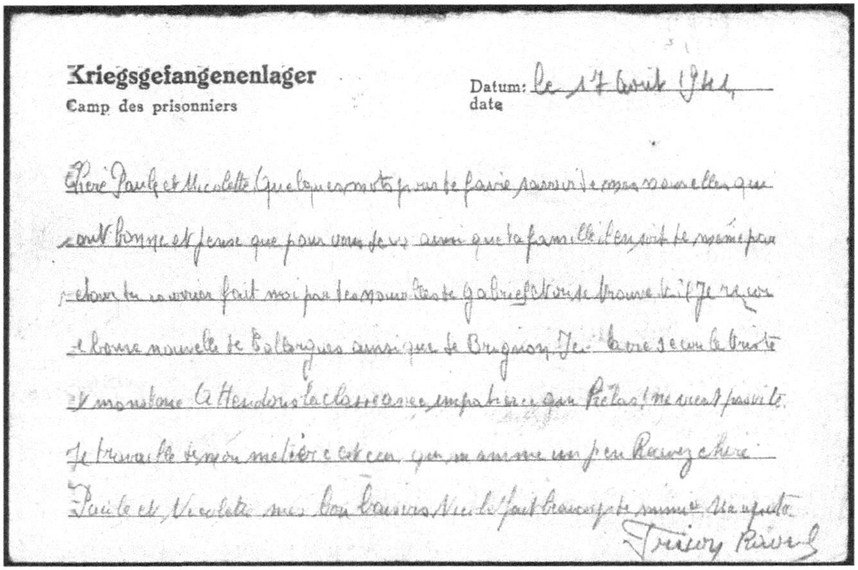
Kriegsgefangenenlager
Camp des prisonniers
Datum: / date:

Figure 8: Front and back of a filled out postcard form, well recognizable the numerated censorship stamp

Figure 9: Mail arrival

Americans, Dutch, and Norwegians, the number of parcels was unlimited, but for the French, Belgians, Poles, and Serbs the number was limited. The norm was to receive two parcels of five kg each per month.[51]

In addition to the parcels from relatives, there were the so-called "love parcels" from private aid organizations. The ICRC, in particular, sent food parcels in large numbers. The food parcels from the ICRC and the other private aid organizations improved the meager and monotonous camp rations with their high-quality food. Most of the packages came from the American Red Cross. The latter sent standard packages containing exactly five kilograms (dried fruit, canned meat and fish, biscuits, cheese, margarine and dried milk, chocolate, cigarettes and soap). Misappropriation of these items by the guards was severely punished. In addition, there were also Red Cross packages with medical supplies and medicines.[52]

The number of incoming parcels was enormous. On average, about 15,000 parcels arrived at Stalag VII A per week around 1940. At Christmas 1940, 150,000 parcels (26 railway wagons full) were sent to the prisoners by relatives, and another 12 wagons by relief organizations. Northwest of the actual camp, on the other side of the Mühlbach, there was a fenced-in "Stalag station" with its own railway siding and a barrack for the parcel post to handle these quantities.[53]

However, the parcels did cause the German military services some headaches in various respects. For example, the distribution of Red Cross parcels varied greatly; US prisoners were by far the best provided for, while Soviet prisoners received hardly any Red Cross parcels, since the ICRC was not approved as an aid organization for them. This also led to the development of a hierarchy in the camp as to who received parcels and who received few or none. Some of those who received frequent parcels and had plenty of food and cigarettes hired other prisoners to do unpopular chores for them. For example, U.S. prisoners sometimes had their latrines cleaned by Soviet prisoners, who were rewarded with food from packages.[54] A black market also developed. According to Colonel Burger, the third camp commandant, up to 100 marks or more were paid for a tin of Nescafé. Although the camp administration tried to stop this black market and insisted that food was to be distributed to the needy, it admitted that it did not succeed.[55]

There was also concern that prohibited items could be smuggled in, especially in private parcels. For that reason, Stalag VII A had detailed regulations on how to deal with parcels in the "Letter and Parcel Post" Service Instruction.

Private parcels were checked intensively and had to be opened in the presence of the recipient, as the recipient had to confirm the contents. In addition, the parcel itself and its contents had to be closely examined in order to prevent the smuggling of prohibited items. For example, canned goods had to be checked for false bottoms, and the seams of clothing had to be scanned. Balls of woolen yarn had to be unwound, and cakes, breads or sausages had to be cut several times.

In addition, the German officers had considerable concern that long-lasting foodstuffs from packages that would not spoil with time, were being hoarded for escape attempts. There were, therefore, instructions not to hand over goods in their original packaging. So even tins of food had to be opened. Jam, dried fruit, coffee, tea or butter could only be handed over in small quantities, and only a fraction of the bar of chocolate. The rest had to be stored.

As the war progressed and the supply situation for the German population became increasingly scarce, goods sent to prisoners that were hardly available to the civilian population, such as chocolate, coffee or cigarettes, led to concerns that attempts at bribery might increase.[56]

The SD ("Sicherheitsdienst", secret service of the SS) mocked the fact that children and youths sought contact with prisoners in order to receive sweets from them. For example, the SD reported an incident in which a British officer on transport placed a bar of chocolate on the table of a station restaurant (In this officer's camp, chocolate was apparently given out in whole bars.) and watched smiling as a group of Germans fought over it. This behavior was undignified, the SD staff noted, and had to be countered with intensified propaganda.[57]

6. Nutrition and clothing

Principles for the catering of prisoners

The German leadership was guided by utilitarian considerations when it came to feeding the prisoners. The rations were to be sufficient to maintain the prisoners' ability to work. At the same time, the diet was not allowed to reach the standard of the German population, otherwise the regime feared unrest. In general, it can be stated that with the increasing supply difficulties in the course of the war, the official rations were cut more and more, and even these amounts were often not completely available, in reality, especially towards the end of the war.

Figure 10: Horse carriages bringing food to the camp are jammed far back on the Thalbacher road in Moosburg. On April 29th,1945 US troups will march into the City of Moosburg via this road.

For propaganda reasons, the British and Americans received the best rations throughout, whereas the rations of Soviet prisoners were barely sufficient for survival in terms of quality and quantity, especially in view of the poor working conditions. In 1944, the Nazi regime also began to feed Soviet prisoners and Italian military internees according to their work performance. Those who met the work standards received full rations, those who did not had their rations cut. This led to a vicious cycle for these prisoner groups. Those who were weakened and, therefore, less able to work, received less rations, which further reduced their performance and, thus, their rations.[58]

Nutrition in the Stalag 1940

An insight into the situation in the early days of the camp is given in a report by the commandant, Colonel Nepf, from January 1941, i.e., when the food situation was still comparatively good and before the arrival of the Soviet prisoners. According to this report, at times 25,000 men had to be fed in the camp, for which 8,000 kg of bread, 2,000 kg of meat, 30,000 kg of potatoes, 300 kg of salt and sugar, and 4,600 kg of other foodstuffs (soup ingredients, cabbage, vegetables, fat, and coffee) were needed per day.[59] It was a simple ration, based mainly on potatoes and bread, fresh vegetables or dairy products were issued sparsely. At the same time, it can be calculated that each prisoner had 320g of bread, 1,200g of potatoes, 80g of meat and about 184g of other food available - not an abundant diet, but sufficient for survival. Western prisoners, in particular, were able to supplement the official rations with food parcels from home. These contained tinned meat and fish, dried fruit, chocolate and coffee and, thus, high-quality food.[60]

The official rations were not weighed out individually and given out to each prisoner separately, but cooked together and then distributed. For breakfast there was substitute coffee made from barley or acorns, for lunch jacket potatoes or stew-like soup, plus the daily bread ration, and in the evening again jacket potatoes. Margarine, among other things, was distributed twice a week. There were canteen kitchens in the Stalag where the meals were prepared. The prisoners were responsible for distributing the food. In addition, prisoners also made small cookers to heat the food from the parcels.[61]

Beer was also supplied to the Stalag. For the 1942/43 business year, it was assumed that the Stalag needed 4,000 hl of beer.[62] In fact, there are pictures showing prisoners in front of the camp's store drinking beer while sitting on beer benches.[63]

Nutrition on work assignment

Depending on the hardness of the work to be done, prisoners on work assignments received food of better quality and quantity than the standard Stalag meals.[64] The prisoners had to be fed by the respective contractor. However, the official rations were not always distributed

Figure 11: Prisoners receiving food under the supervision of German guards

in full, since sometimes parts of the food were diverted for bonuses or for other parts of the workforce.[65]

Leaflets from 1942 and 1943 show that the nutrition issue was primarily concerned with maintaining the labor force. The companies that employed prisoners were asked to ensure adequate nutrition: Every hour of work lost due to malnutrition is lost to the national economy.[66]

For the prisoners of Stalag VII A on work duty, there were general guidelines for nutrition. Meat was to be given, if possible, in the form of "Freibankfleisch" (low-quality meat that was not approved for general sale) or horse meat, and a fat portion such as margarine. "For Soviet Russians, it is recommended that satiating soups are prepared, that correspond to the dietary habits of the POW, giving 360 g of rye flour, or 380 g of rye meal, or 360 g of rye groats, instead of 500 g of bread." At the same time, this leaflet required the companies to draw up weekly menus in "the simplest form" so that the prisoners' diets could be monitored. In addition, the leaflet called on the employer to avoid any "health-disrupting uniformity" in the composition of food and to design varied menus. To this end, they were also to plant "spice gardens" in which to grow leeks, parsley, chervil or garlic.[67]

The prisoners who were on work duty for the City of Moosburg were supplied by Moosburg inns, to which the town made available food coupons it had received for feeding the prisoners.[68]

Different diets for different groups of prisoners

For Soviet prisoners, the situation was fundamentally different. Only when it was decided in the fall of 1941 to bring Soviet prisoners into the Reich for work were they granted rations sufficient to survive from December 1941 on.[69] But even after this change of mind, the Soviet soldiers remained third-class prisoners after the Western Allies, Yugoslavs, and Poles, and were the worst fed.[70]

When the rations for Germans had to be reduced in April 1942, the lower rations for Soviet prisoners were also reduced to maintain the old gap, for normal workers from 2,540 calories to 2,070. However, in view of the mostly heavy physical work that Soviet prisoners had to perform, the new rations were too low, so that in early October the rate had to be increased to 2,283 calories. In the 1940s, nutritional physiologists assumed that 1,800-2,000 calories per day would be needed for basic metabolism and minimal physical exercise, and 2,400 calories by normal consumers.

A comparison of the ration rates between Germans, non-Soviet and Soviet prisoners is particularly interesting. When deployed in the industrial economy,

Figure 12: Food was brought from the kitchens to the prisoners in large tin buckets.

the following rations per week were fixed for heavy laborers in October 1943: Meat: Germans 600g, non-Soviet POW 480g, Soviet POW 400g; Fat: Germans 319g, non-Soviet POW 283g, Soviet POW 200g; Bread: Germans 3,825g, non-Soviet POW 3,350g, Soviet POW, however, 3,750g. In addition, the quality of the food also differed. For example, at times there was a special "Russian bread" baked from rye meal, sugar beet pulp, cell flour, straw flour and leaves.[71]

The main reason for the high mortality rate among the Soviet prisoners, also in Stalag VII A, was this completely inadequate nutrition. The Soviet prisoners suffered from constant hunger. They tried to make do by stealing food, begging or exchanging handcrafted children's toys for bread.[72]

Clothing

The clothing situation of the prisoners was problematic throughout. At first, the prisoners of war kept the clothes they had worn when they were captured. In some cases, they arrived at the camp in more or less ragged uniforms after front-line duty, their stay in the transit camp and the long transports. Sufficient replacement clothing was not available. The number of captured uniforms was never sufficient to clothe prisoners anew and to compensate for the wear and tear during the often years-long imprisonment. The supply of shoes was particularly difficult. Leather shoes could hardly be replaced. In 1942, 75% of the prisoners had no leather shoes.[73]

While Western prisoners received replacements via clothing parcels from home, this route was not open to Soviet prisoners and Italian military internees. The lack of clothing, especially underwear, led to considerable hygienic problems against the background of the poor sanitary conditions in the prisoners' quarters. Vermin infestation in the barracks of these prisoner groups occurred regularly; often Soviet and Italian prisoners had lice.[74]

The Stalag set up a tailor shop and a shoemaker's workshop to provide relief. In January 1941, 99 prisoners were working in the Stalag tailor shop and 315 captured French and Poles in the shoemaker's workshop. In the autumn of 1940, work was done there seven days a week, and on a single Sunday 700 pairs of shoes were mended. The prisoners were also required to maintain their clothing in a weekly cleaning and mending session.[75]

Figure 13: Prisoners mending clothes

In addition, the shortage was managed in detail and meticulously. The leaders of the work detachments had to report in detail on the stock of clothing. For this purpose, the multi-page form "Statement 'A' on the total stock of POW clothing in the command" (Nachweisung 'A' über den Gesamtbestand an Kgf.-Bekleidung im Kommando) had to be filled out and sent to the Stalag on a monthly basis. The stock of caps, cloth jackets, cloth trousers, coats, neckbands, leather boots and leather shoes, wooden shoes, wooden slippers, stockings or foot rags, shirts, undershirts and sports shirts, undershorts, drill jackets, drill trousers, work jackets, work trousers, work coats, "Bolshevik shirts" and cotton jackets, gaiters, underjackets, blankets, towels, handkerchiefs, gloves, head and ear protectors, woolen scarves, steel helmets and gas masks were to be listed.[76] In addition to this, there was also a filling-in instruction of the size of a typewriter page, in which it was explained what was to be understood by the individual categories.[77] In addition, the leaders of the work detachments had to keep a "clothing record" for each prisoner, listing all the items of clothing that the prisoner had received.[78] If an item of clothing was lost or damaged, the Stalag had to be informed and the reason for the loss or damage also given.[79]

The prisoners were provided with two blankets made of "coarse yarn"; there was no bedding. In unfavorable conditions, for example if the accommodation could not be heated, the prisoners could also receive a third blanket. In March 1942, it was ordered that paper blankets be issued to Soviet prisoners, alledgedly for hygienic reasons.[80]

7. Prisoner of war labor

Based on the positive experiences in the First World War, the German leadership planned from the beginning to use prisoners of war for labor as much as possible. According to the Geneva Convention, captured enlisted men were obliged to perform work as long as it did not involve occupations that were harmful to their health or activities directly related to the war effort. Non-commissioned officers could decide for themselves whether they wanted to work.[81]

That prisoners of war were seen primarily as a labor force is shown by a passage from a Wehrmacht General Command (OKW) leaflet for guards dated January 1943: "Prisoners of war are laborers of the German Reich who must be fully utilized for the German economy during the war." For the benefit of the German people, the labor force of the prisoners of war had to be maintained. This included adequate housing, sufficient rations, and proper and correct treatment.[82]

The POW was, thus, not to be treated properly for his own sake, but only to the extent that he was needed as a labor force.

Work assignment in agriculture and industry

The very first Polish prisoners who arrived in the camps in the Reich in the late autumn of 1939 were to be used for agricultural work, especially for harvesting potatoes and beets and, thus, replace the agricultural workers who had been drafted into the Wehrmacht. As a result, 300,000 Polish prisoners of war were actually working in

Figure 14: French prisoners working in farming

agriculture as early as 1939.[83] As late as September 1939, the command of the military district instructed the administration of Stalag VII A to ensure that the prisoners were quickly put to work harvesting potatoes and beets.[84] Therefore, most of the Polish prisoners stayed in the Stalag for only a short time at first.

From 1940 onwards, prisoners were also increasingly used in mining, construction and industry, as there was also a shortage of workforce there. As the war continued, the need for labor in agriculture and industry increased. Skilled workers were also increasingly drafted and replaced by prisoners of war.[85]

Figure 15: Polish prisoners at work

Organization and scope of work

In order to better coordinate the use of labor and to identify skilled workers and specialists among the prisoners, there were labor offices in the Stalags, including Moosburg.

Employers requested the prisoners from the Stalag Labor Office. The companies and the German Reich, represented by the Stalag, then signed a contract for the transfer of prisoners.[86] The assignment of prisoners was not an employment relationship under civil law, but a legal relationship of its own kind under public law. In March 1942, the OKW instructed the Stalag commandant offices not to execute any more transfer contracts in the future, for reasons of simplification, but to inform the contractor of the applicable regulations in a leaflet when transferring the prisoners. The employer of the prisoners, paid compensation per day and prisoner to the Stalag and had also to provide room and board.[87]

A few figures show the extent to which the prisoners were used as laborers. On September 10, 1940, of 62,768 prisoners in the area of Stalag VII A, 34,022 were assigned to work detachments; on January 10, 1941, of 55,130 prisoners, 43,177 were already assigned to work detachments; on January 1, 1942, of 59,169 prisoners, 53,301 were assigned to work detachments; on January 1, 1943, 57,325 of 65,771 were assigned to work detachments; on January 1, 1944, 54,932 of 74,096 prisoners were still assigned to work detachments; and on December 1, 1944 (the last available list), of 75,400 prisoners, 56,350 were still assigned to work detachments.[88]

Subcamps

Against this background, for most prisoners the Stalag in Moosburg was merely a transit station, from where they were distributed to work detachments in the area of the military district. If the distance between the Stalag and the place of deployment was too far to be covered daily, the prisoners were placed in subcamps at the place of work. There were numerous such subcamps in the area of military district VII, which were organizationally assigned to Stalag VII A. The prisoners returned to the Stalag when they fell ill or when they had completed their mission and had not yet been sent on their next assignment.[89]

The Stalag issued instructions as to how the satellite camps were to be constructed. They had to be fenced in with 2.5 m high barbed wire, the windows had to be barred and the doors had to be lockable. If prisoners were allowed to spend the night individually at the site, the contractor had to remove their pants and shoes in the evening and lock them up separately.[90]

Payment

Of the compensation that the contractor had to pay to the Stalag, a part was credited or paid to the prisoner. The payment was made in camp money to avoid escape attempts.[91] With the camp money, the prisoners could buy food in the camp's own canteen, and in some cases, they were also allowed to transfer this money home. Inspired by Stalag VII B (Memmingen), an appeal appeared in one issue of the camp newspaper to establish a relief organization for the benefit of needy families of French prisoners. At least 50 Pf (Pfennig) per month were to be given from the wages. The German authorities supported the project and a first collection

Figure 16: A group of prisoners with a German guard on the way to the work assignment

yielded 850 RM (Reichsmark), a second one already 2,210 RM.[92]

The remuneration of prisoners depended on the sector in which they were employed and also changed repeatedly. In industry, for example, the minimum wage for a prisoner as of November 1943 was 50 Pf. per day, for a Soviet 25 Pf. Mostly, however, the earnings were higher, so that a non-Soviet prisoner earned 16 RM per week, and a Soviet 8 RM, compared to 51 RM average wage of a German industrial worker. In some cases, employers were also allowed to pay performance incentives.[93]

When, during the war, the guarding of the prisoners became looser and looser due to a lack of personnel, opportunities opened up for them to earn extra money. On Saturday afternoons or Sundays, for example, they could earn a few Reichsmarks on the side. Especially for Soviet prisoners, this additional work on farms was an important opportunity to get additional food. However, this sideline work also repeatedly brought the prisoners into conflict with their employers, since the prisoners spared their strength in order to be able to do the extra work.

Prisoners employed in industry also had the opportunity to make toys out of material waste and sell them.[94] However, this was forbidden and could even be dangerous. The management of an industrial plant in the area of Stalag VII A, dissatisfied with the performance of its Soviet prisoners, called the crafting of toys from scrap metal sabotage under the "War Special Punishment Ordinance" (Wehrkraftschutz-verordnung) and demanded that the Ministry of Armaments, the responsible POW commander, and the Gestapo office in Munich shoot some of the "saboteurs" in front of the assembled crew in order to stop this "sabotage".[95]

Working conditions

Prisoners of war were to be treated like German workers as far as breaks or overtime were concerned. They were not to be better off. However, this also meant that the right to breaks, which the Geneva Convention demanded, was not always implemented. As German workers also had to work seven days a week in emergencies, so did the prisoners of war. This could result in the elimination of days off per week required by the Geneva Convention. If civilian workers had to work overtime, so did the prisoners of war.[96]

In daily practice, working conditions varied greatly by nation. Due to National Socialist ideology, Soviet prisoners and Italian military internees had the worst positions. The latter were considered traitors by the German public after Italy's armistice with the Allies in 1943. Members of these two groups were assigned to the most unpleasant, difficult, and dangerous work. When German superiors beat these prisoners, in many cases the military authorities did not intervene. At the

other end of the scale, were the Anglo-American prisoners. They enjoyed almost the complete protection of the Geneva Convention. Criticism of food, housing and working conditions was often voiced confidently without fear of repression. This also applied to slow work. Western prisoners were also rarely beaten. They were often able to gain the recognition of their German colleagues, especially if they were skilled workers.[97]

Surveillance during the work assignment

The regular guard crews could not take over the guarding of the prisoners on the numerous field commands. Therefore, upon request, if the local police authority raised no objections, civilians were assigned by the district administrator or from the Stalag as "auxiliary guards" to guard the prisoners on work detail. When prisoners were individually assigned to a farmer or craftsman, no guard accompanied them, but the German farmer or craftsman was appointed "auxiliary guard" with the appropriate powers.[98] The guard's task, in addition to guarding the prisoners, was to protect the German people from harm. It was especially important to those in charge that the guards also ensured that the prisoners gave their fullest effort in their work. The guards were to set an inspiring example through their eager committment.[99]

Work assignments in Moosburg

Already in September 1939, when the considerations of the Wehrmacht for the construction of a prison camp became known, the City of Moosburg planned to use prisoners for public works.[100] The Moosburg municipal building department and the German Reich, represented by the commandant of Stalag VII A, therefore, made a corresponding contract on November

15, 1939, with effect as early as November 14, 1939. The town received 20 unskilled workers for road construction.[101] In the following years, the town continuously employed prisoners. In the summer and fall of 1940, Philipp Holzmann AG built the city's main sewer. Between 11 and 79 prisoners were employed for this construction project from August 19 to November 2.[102] In April 1941, 50 prisoners were made available to the city "for work in progress."[103] In December 1943, and January 1944, the town used prisoners in the construction of makeshift homes, and in August 1943 also in the construction of splinter protection trenches.[104] In October 1944, the municipality of Moosburg employed 168 prisoners (guarded by five guards).[105]

Numerous prisoners were also employed in the private sector in Moosburg and the surrounding area, distributed among various commands. A list dated 07.11.1942, gives the following figures: agriculture and trade 105 prisoners, industry and construction 211, in the villages of Niederambach 42, Bruckberg 20, Thonstetten 14, Mauern 34, Oberhummel 15, Inkofen 16, Reichersdorf 65 and Aich 32.[106]

8. Contact of prisoners of war with the German civilian population

Contact ban

The contact of prisoners of war with the civilian population was most undesirable by the German leadership as it was considered to be potentially dangerous.[107] The various fears can be seen in a leaflet issued by the OKW (Wehrmacht General Command) in

1943: "Any contact beyond what is necessary is forbidden, not only because it is incompatible with the honor and pride of a German, but also because there is a danger of spying on things that are important to the war effort or because it can cause harm to the "national comrades" (Volksgenossen) in terms of demographic policy."[108]

The regime, therefore, used propaganda, bans and punishments to prevent contacts between prisoners and German civilians.

Section 4 of the "War Special Punishment Ordinance" (Wehrkraftschutzverordnung) of 1939 stipulated that prohibited contact with prisoners could be punished. This meant the violation of a regulation for dealing with prisoners or contact with prisoners that "grossly offends the public common sense."

As early as November 1939, however, reports were available "from which it can be seen that this attitude toward an enemy of the people is not being adopted everywhere."[109] Above all, the local NSDAP leaders were instructed to act against this behavior. Each contact between "Volksgenossen" and prisoners of war was to be prevented by order or, if that did not succeed, by police measures.[110]

The NSDAP district leader of Freising obviously took this request to heart and complained to the district administrator on October 21, 1940, about the fact that a Moosburg inn was frequented by French doctors who had been imprisoned (and who were allowed to move about freely to a certain extent) "[It is] unworthy of a German that he entertains prisoners".[111]

Propaganda measures and bans

In the years that followed, there were numerous decrees and campaigns by party committees, civilian authorities, and military departments to establish in the minds of the population that prisoners of war continued to be enemies of the German people and were to be treated as such.

In May 1940, a circular issued by the Reich Minister of the Interior stipulated that all contact and relationships with prisoners of war were forbidden, unless this could not be avoided due to an employment relationship or a service obligation. But even then, contact with prisoners was to be limited to the most necessary extent. Cases of undesirable contact with prisoners were now expressly punishable. This applied to numerous everyday situations, such as forwarding mail and written or oral communications bypassing camp censorship, exchanging money, buying and selling, exchanging or donating objects of any kind, especially stamps, money, ink or alcohol, talking or giving a radio.[112]

Another leaflet from 1940 says: "If you treat them like Germans or even better, you will become traitors to the national community ... Do not let the prisoners of war sit at the table with you. They do not belong to the home or farm community, much less to the family... Prisoners of war have no place at festivals and celebrations. For we want to be among ourselves at our celebrations and family feasts."[113] Going to church together was forbidden, as was going to pubs together. For example, a Moosburg confectioner was deprived of his POW because he had taken him to the cemetery on All Saints' Day.[114]

Police custody and job loss

Violations of these regulations were punished. This applied above all to aiding escape, unauthorized transmission of messages, and all actions that were likely to facilitate sabotage and espionage by prisoners of war. The judiciary was instructed to crack down.

Gauleiters (regional leaders of the Nazi Party) were advised to publish in their bulletins court sentences for forbidden dealings with prisoners. Statistics from the judiciary and the Gestapo show that there were hundreds of cases of forbidden intercourse between civilians and prisoners.[115]

Thus, from January 3 to 7, 1940, the Munich Gestapo office also carried out an action in Moosburg for forbidden dealings with prisoners of war. Six Moosburg residents were arrested, including two women who had spoken to prisoners in an inn and accepted drinks and cigarettes from them. The Gestapo also arrested a photographer who had taken pictures of prisoners. Arrest warrants were applied against these persons.[116]

In contrast, a municipal employee was almost lucky, she only lost her job because of contact with prisoners. An employee of the municipal treasurer's office reported to the mayor that on April 4, 1942, at about two o'clock, he had noticed that a municipal office employee had been talking to two French prisoners in the office of the municipal building department. The latter had been sitting in their chairs smoking cigarettes and with folded arms and had smiled. He had learned that the office assistant had been in the building office since half past two o'clock. He further wrote: "When one knows the condition in which our soldiers arrive here in the hospital trains, and when one has to hear from the "Landesschützen" (guardsmen) that our soldiers are still being laughed at by the prisoners of war, then one will conclude that it is high time that these conditions in the building office are abolished as soon as possible." He further stated that the two prisoners were no longer needed, as no one was in a position to control their activities. It was certainly not right for the two prisoners to sit alone in the construction office, left to their own devices.

Mayor Müller ordered that the employment relationship with the office worker be terminated immediately, and the two French engineers were to return to the camp after completing their work.[117]

Forbidden love affairs with prisoners

The regime's entire concern was for German women. "The German woman, in particular, must be aware that she must not enter into any relationship with the prisoners of war. Otherwise, she will lose her most precious asset, her honor. German woman, therefore, also avoid all false appearances."[118] In 1943, women were admonished: "German women who enter into relations with prisoners of war exclude themselves from the "folk community" ("Volksgemeinschaft") and will receive their just punishment. Even the appearance of rapprochement must be avoided."[119]

Love affairs between German women and prisoners of war also fell under the "War Special Punishment Ordinance" (Wehrkraftschutzverordnung) and were punished by the courts. In Military District VII, the command of military district announced sentences against German women for relationships with Polish prisoners of war in a letter dated January 1940. Every businessman who employed prisoners of war and the local mayor received a copy of the notice. In addition, the command of the military district ordered the camp administration to inform the guards that they would be severely punished if they allowed German women to have relations with prisoners.[120] The Landesschützen battalion 512, which was responsible for guarding the prisoners, also strongly impressed this on the guard crews in a circular from 1943.[121]

The camp regulations of Stalag VII A of January 8, 1944 also forbade (in paragraph 1!) prisoners of war to approach German women and threatened those committing an infraction with imprisonment and, with reference to the War Special Punishment Ordinance, with the death penalty.[122]

Numerous contacts in everyday life

The recurring campaigns and the numerous decrees, leaflets and notices, as well as the statistics of the Gestapo and the judiciary, show that there were, after all, numerous and intensive contacts between the German civilian population and prisoners of war. The use of prisoners for work, which was becoming increasingly widespread, resulted in countless situations that made contact between prisoners and civilians possible. Thus, in industrial plants or in construction, prisoners and German civilian workers worked together in shifts. Particularly close relationships could develop on farms or in craft enterprises, to which individual prisoners were assigned, often for longer periods, as substitutes for conscripted journeymen or farmhands. These prisoners often spent the night there and received their rations. Here, the prisoners inevitably took part in the daily life of the family. According to Colonel Burger, camp commandant 1943-1945, the prisoners in these cases were sometimes treated like family members.[123] For example, the SD ("Sicherheitsdienst" - Secret Service of the SS) reported as early as November 1939 that it had happened that Polish prisoners who had been assigned to farmers for harvest work were taken into the family by them. Polish prisoners also went to church with the farmers with whom they had been assigned.[124] The Landesschützenbattalion 512 also demanded in a circular letter to the labor commands of February 22, 1943: "5. In areas where prisoners of war are treated too familiarly on farms, a change is to be arranged in consultation with the labor offices before the spring work begins."[125]

It also happened time and again that employer gave food as gifts to the prisoners they employed. In August 1942, the Moosburg business owners had to sign a form that indicated that they were aware of the ban on giving gifts to prisoners, as well as the fact that a violation could have penal consequences.[126]

Prohibition of approaching the camp

The camp administration also tried to prevent prisoners of war from coming into contact with civilians as much as possible. The very location of the compound outside the city facilitated this. Civilians were only allowed to enter the camp with a permit from the General Command of the Wehrmacht and under the guidance of an escort. Requests for this privilege had to be submitted in writing to the camps' headquarters. Visitors had to sign in and out at the camps' headquarters when entering and leaving the camp. Even those who had permission to enter the camp were not allowed to contact prisoners. This was forbidden under penalty of law. Women and children could not visit the camp. One was only allowed to approach the camp fence from a distance of 100 meters. The reason given for this was "possible danger during measures to prevent escape attempts." The camp administration feared that the use of firearms against escapees could endanger civilians in this way.[127]

The fact that these regulations were not consistently observed is clear from eyewitness accounts. For example, children traded toys made by Soviet prisoners for bread through the camp's barbed wire fence.

9. Pastoral care and leisure activities

Pastoral care for prisoners of war

There was no psychological care for the prisoners in the Stalags. Much of what psychologists do today in similar situations was done by clergy in the POW camps of World War II. Therefore, their activities were of great importance for the prisoners.

Figure 17: Prisoners during the Corpus Christi procession

Detailed information is available on the pastoral care in Stalag VII A, especially for the large number of Catholic prisoners. Prof. Dr. Ziegler, who cared for prisoners in the area of Military District VII as a Catholic clergyman, has described his experiences in detail.[128] First of all, Ziegler describes the great importance of spiritual assistance for the prisoners. They were imprisoned for an indefinite period in a very confined space, without privacy. In addition, according to Prof. Dr. Ziegler, there was downright traumatization because of the rapid German victories and the worry about relatives, with whom there was often no contact for weeks. Ziegler suspects that this is why the Polish prisoners in particular took up the religious offer so intensively. He writes that the rush to the services was enormous.[129]

At first, there was no Polish priest in the camp in Moosburg, since in Poland clergymen were exempt from military service. Therefore, Prof. Dr. Ziegler, who knew the Polish language, initially began to hold services exclusively for Polish prisoners. On December 14, 1939, he celebrated his first mass in the canteen tent with an improvised altar. This service was attended by several thousand prisoners. At Christmas, 1939, Prof. Dr. Ziegler heard the confession of 930 prisoners. In the St. John's Church in Moosburg (which was repeatedly used by prisoners in the years to come), services were held for the Polish soldiers on both of the two Christmas holidays.[130]

Figure 18: Corpus Christi procession

At times, in 1940, there were 130 French priests in the camp, all of whom celebrated on Sundays. On Sundays and holidays, there were services for Poles and French at 8, 9 and 10 o'clock. There was not enough space for a joint large service. On Sunday afternoons, there were devotions, "Vesper" and "Complet". On Sundays, the clergy administered Communion an average of 700 times, and 1800 times on Christmas Day 1940. That year, French clergymen celebrated Christmas Mass at 7 p.m. simultaneously in all 42 barracks of the camp. This had been organized by a captain of the camp administration.[131]

Particularly impressive were the solemn Corpus Christi services with subsequent processions, in which several thousand prisoners took part and which lasted about two hours. The prisoners had set up elaborate altars with rich floral decorations, and the parish of Moosburg lent liturgical equipment and vestments. Choirs and music groups of the prisoners accompanied the services and processions with music and singing.[132]

There were also individual baptisms and the celebration of First Communion in the camp, as well as the administration of Confirmation. In some cases, the clergy performed long-distance weddings for French prisoners. If Catholic prisoners died, they were blessed and buried according to the Catholic rite.[133]

In the beginning, the services were celebrated in a large tent, and in fine weather also outdoors. Prof. Dr. Ziegler's plan to build a chapel in the camp was not approached by the camp administration, although Prof. Dr. Ziegler wanted to build it with church funds. Instead, the commandant made a barrack available for church services. The camp library was housed in an adjoining room. The equipment of altars, cult utensils, altar linen and benches were gradually acquired with the help of various agencies. The French priests who had been imprisoned received small mess kits from France containing all the necessities, and artists among the prisoners painted the pictures. Due to a short circuit in the camp library, the church barrack burned down on Sunday, May 23, 1943; only part of the inventory could be saved.[134]

A highlight of religious life in the Stalag was the visit of the Apostolic Nuncio to Germany, Cesare Orsenigo, Titular Archbishop of Ptolemais, on Sunday, January 26, 1941 - one of the few visits of the Nuncio to German prison camps ever.[135] The church barrack was festively decorated with pictures of the Stations of the Cross painted especially for this purpose. The Mass, supposedly permitted by special order of Hitler, was accompanied by a large prisoners' choir and a prisoners' orchestra. They performed a specially composed mass, the "Messe de Captivité".[136]

Religious services were only permitted for the work commands if the work did not have to be done on Sundays because of urgent tasks, if sufficient guards were available, and if contact with the German civilian population was ruled out.[137]

From May 1941 onwards, German clergy were almost completely forbidden to hold religious services for prisoners of war. Prisoner priests were to take over this task as much as possible.

Priests who ministered to prisoners were strictly supervised. Sermons and funeral orations were subject to pre-censorship by the camp's counterintelligence officer. An interpreter from the camp's Counter-intelligence Group attended church services and funerals. For religious services, the clergy were only allowed to use the sermon liturgy templates approved by the General Command of the Wehrmacht (OKW). Bibles, prayer books and religious writings could only be distributed to prisoners if this had been approved by the OKW.[138]

The growing number of prisoners of non-Catholic Christian denominations and other religions also received pastoral care during the course of the war. For the Catholic-Ukrainian prisoners, a priest from Munich and an interpreter employed in the camp, who was also a priest, celebrated religious services. At times, there was also a Serbian military priest in the camp, who had an altar in a separate part of a barrack. The Protestant town priest from Freising looked after the Protestants, mainly British and Americans. An Anglican clergyman, accompanied by an interpreter, was able to visit work detachments and hold services there. The Soviet prisoners had their own chapel, which they decorated with folk art. Muslims, Sikhs, Hindus and soldiers from the colonies could also practice their religions. They, too, had their own places of worship. In the camp, there were Buddhist priests and Brahmins, among others.[139]

Cultural life

The camp administration tried to support cultural activities of the prisoners in order to keep them busy and distract them a little from their situation. The French prisoners were particularly active in this respect. They ran a theater group and an orchestra. The theatre performed plays by Racine, Kleist, Moliere and Shaw, while the orchestra performed works from all eras.[140]

Figure 19: Prisoner orchestra

In 1942, under the guidance of the French sculptor Antoniucci Voltigero (known as Volti, 1915-1989), French artists created a sculpture to commemorate their time in the camp. It features four reliefs representing the four largest rivers in France (Loire, Rhône, Seine, Garonne). In 1963, the City of Moosburg completed it to a fountain and erected a memorial in the Moosburg city district Neustadt, in memory of Stalag VII A.

The French published a camp newspaper once a week, *"Trait d`union,"*[141] which offered insights into cultural life in the camp and extensive sports coverage. This newspaper was even sent to outlying commands. French prisoners had also established a camp university, whose library contained 11,000 books and periodicals, but it fell victim to the barracks fire described above. Lectures suffered from the fact that only very limited space was available and that learners and teachers were repeatedly dispersed to work detachments. Nevertheless, after the war, the Sorbonne University in Paris recognized credits from the camp university.

But the prisoners of other nationalities also developed cultural activities. The British, for example, maintained an orchestra. Its members were even uniformly dressed, with shirt and bow tie. Yugoslavs performed plays, with elaborate sets at their disposal. Soviet prisoners performed folk dances and folk songs in one of their living barracks. Educational opportunities were available for American prisoners. Courses were offered for them in accounting, mathematics, Spanish, French, and German, among other subjects.

Stand-up concerts and open-air theatre performances took place time and again, and comedians also performed. In general, it is noticeable that the theatre groups were able to draw on an astonishingly rich range of props and costumes. Some of the necessary materials were provided by the International Committee of the Red Cross (ICRC).

There were also painters and draftsmen among the prisoners. Many of their works, portraits of fellow prisoners, scenes from life in the camp and caricatures, have survived. The prisoners also organized exhibitions of paintings, drawings and watercolors, as well as detailed and lovingly-crafted models depicting buildings or everyday situations from home.

In contrast to captured officers, who did not have to work, the ordinary soldiers captured in the Stalag had only limited time and energy for cultural activities in addition to their work assignments. This was especially true of Soviet prisoners, who used their little free time to make the small toys, which they exchanged for food.

Sports

The OKW attached great importance to sports activities in the camps as physical exercise for those prisoners who were not on work duty.[142] In Stalag VII A there was an astonishingly wide range of sports activities. A

Figure 20: Racing

Figure 2¯: Boxing match

relatively-large part of the camp grounds was taken up by the so-called "sports and playground." Here, the prisoners played football and rugby, among other things. In addition, numerous pictures have survived documenting the playing of other sports. There was tennis, whereby it is noted that the prisoners played in proper tennis clothing with apparently high-quality rackets. This can be explained by the fact that Western prisoners could also have sports equipment sent from home. American prisoners played volleyball and basketball. They even organized a baseball league. In the winter, there was also the possibility of ice skating. Chess was another popular pastime; many pictures show prisoners engrossed in the game of kings.

Sports festivals with music and parades were also held in the Stalag. Boxing matches and races were organized, which aroused great interest among the prisoners.[143]

10. Medical care and death of prisoners

The medical care a camp inmate received depended on his nationality. While Western prisoners received relatively good treatment, Soviet soldiers initially received hardly any medical care. Only when Soviet prisoners of war were urgently needed for work did they receive a minimum of medical care. However, its standard was significantly lower than that for other prisoners and was purely geared to maintaining manpower.

This also affected the mortality rate, which was by far the highest among Soviet prisoners.

Even in death, prisoners were not equal, as evidenced by the different burial regulations depending on nationality.

Medical care

The camp doctor had the most important function in the medical care of the prisoners. He was responsible, like a medical officer, for health care, medical treatment, the hygienic supervision of the camp and the implementation of the related measures. The entire medical staff of the camp was subordinate to him, also from a disciplinary point of view. He supervised both the camp kitchen and the delousing operations and was also required to inspect the barracks on a regular basis. The treatment of prisoners in the infirmaries and camp hospitals was carried out by prisoner-of-war doctors and paramedics; the camp doctor merely supervised.[144]

There were several sick quarters in the Stalag. Mainly paramedics took care of minor illnesses and injuries there. At the end of 1940, there were three such stations in the camp, visited daily by 300 to 600 prisoners. More serious cases were taken to the camp hospital. Prisoners who had fallen seriously ill or had suffered more serious injuries during their work outside the camp were also taken there. The camp hospital had about 1000 beds and modern equipment. Six prisoner doctors, sixteen medics and fifty helpers treated the patients. The camp doctor had three other German doctors under him. In

Figure 22: Nurses deployed in the Stalag

addition, a German and a French dentist took care of the prisoners. In general, there was no shortage of medical personnel in the Stalag. By the end of 1940, there were about 2000 doctors and medics in the Stalag VII A area. The camp hospital took up almost a quarter of the camp area and was separated from the rest of the camp by its own barbed wire fence. Separated again from the actual hospital area was a small area with isolation barracks for infectious diseases.[145]

If treatment in the camp hospital was not sufficient, the prisoners were sent to a Wehrmacht hospital or to a special clinic. The prisoners from Moosburg were usually taken to the reserve hospital (as Wehrmacht hospitals in the homeland were called) on the Domberg in Freising. In principle, prisoners and Wehrmacht soldiers were to be treated strictly separately. Only in emergencies, for example, in the case of acute illnesses or accidents during the work assignment, or if a specialist was needed, did prisoners receive the necessary medical care in civilian hospitals or on an outpatient basis from civilian doctors.[146]

Because of the close quarters and the sometimes problematic hygienic conditions, skin diseases such as scabies occurred relatively often, as did infectious diseases. Hernias also seem to have been frequent, as there were detailed instructions on how to treat them. The camp occasionally had to contend with epidemics of dysentery, typhus and tuberculosis.[147]

In order to prevent illnesses and epidemics, the camp doctor ordered various precautionary measures to be taken by those who employed prisoners in labor. For example, he demanded that the contractors provide the prisoners with a sufficient and varied diet. The kitchen staff had to submit a stool sample once a year to the hygienic examination office of Military District VII. In addition, he instructed the commanders to provide sufficient facilities for personal hygiene and for cleaning clothing, and to ensure scrupulous cleanliness and adequate heating of the accommodations. In the event that vermin appeared, there were precise instructions on how to combat them.[148]

If a prisoner was ill or injured, the treatments that were to be carried out were primarily those that served to quickly restore the ability to work. Vaccinations against tuberculosis, typhus and paratyphoid fever, for example, were only given in the prisoner-of-war camps when it was feared that such epidemics might delay or hinder the prisoners' work. Dental prostheses could also be granted to a prisoner, but only if the ability to work was impaired and the corps physician of the command of Military District VII had approved. Visually-impaired prisoners received ophthalmological care and eyeglasses.[149]

The fact that the preservation of the labor force was the primary goal of medical treatment becomes particularly clear in the situation of the Soviet prisoners. It was only when they were urgently needed for work that a reasonably-effective medical care system was established for them, even if only on a limited scale. Vaccines against tuberculosis, for example, which had their origin in the "Russian camps", were not made available to the Soviet prisoners, although they were the main victims of this disease.[150]

Deaths among prisoners

If prisoners died in the camp, German doctors performed a post-mortem examination and sent the death certificate with details of the cause of death to the registry office in Moosburg, which then issued a death certificate. The Stalag had to be informed in the case of deaths in the subcamps. The Stalag administration then informed the Wehrmacht Information Center for War Casualties and Prisoners of War in Berlin and the International Committee of the Red Cross in Geneva (except in the case of deaths of Soviet prisoners). These offices, in turn, informed the relatives. This system functioned until shortly before the end of the war; the last death certificate was received by the City of Moosburg on April 23, 1945.[151]

The number of those who died in the Stalag is difficult to determine. The official death list of the Stalag, in which the deaths were documented up to the last day before the liberation of the camp, has disappeared

Figure 23: Gravesite at the POW cemetery in Oberreit

according to current knowledge.[152] Various lists exist, but their numbers differ considerably. A chronological list (1939 to mid-April 1945) lists 860 deaths. An alphabetical list (September 1, 1939- April 29, 1945) lists 745 known deaths and 25 unknown deaths. A list dated June 18, 1946, indicates 908 deaths. This last list is problematic in that it includes civilians.[153] A list from 1984 gives the number of 987 burials in the Oberreit POW cemetery.[154] However, it is unclear whether all of these persons actually died in the Stalag. There are contemporary witness reports according to which mainly Soviet prisoners did not survive the transport to Moosburg and were then buried in Oberreit. In addition, civilians and those who died after the camp was dissolved were also buried in the POW cemetery. Colonel Burger, camp commandant from 1943-1945, cites the number of prisoners who died in the Stalag as 917, 700 of them Soviet soldiers, 400 of whom died soon after arriving in the camp. According to Burger, 300 prisoners killed in air raids outside the camp should be added to the figure of 917. An analysis of index cards of Soviet prisoners reveales, that at least 1065 Soviet prisoners died in Stalag VII A or its subcamps.[155]

One thing, however, can be gleaned from all the lists. If one breaks down the figures by nationality and cause of death, the catastrophic situation of the Soviet prisoners becomes clear.

Thus, 29 British[156] and 11 American prisoners died[157], while in Oberreit about 700[158] Soviet prisoners were buried, some of whose names are unknown. In addition, 48 French[159] , 22 Italians[160] and 17 Poles, among others, lost their lives in the camp. The number of Yugoslavs who died varies between 42 and 58, depending on the list.[161]

The causes of death also clearly show the different living conditions of the various prisoner groups. Of the British prisoners, six died in 1943, ten in 1944 and 13 in 1945. The causes of death varied: tuberculosis, scarlet fever, cancer, circulatory failure, diphtheria, gunshot wounds and suicide. One died after drinking methylated spirits. Three British were killed on March 13,1945 near the village of Marzling during an air raid. It can be assumed that they were shot at by Allied low-flying aircraft, whose pilots did not recognize the prisoners as such.[162] The causes of death of the eleven deceased American soldiers are similar: suicide, jaundice, diphtheria (multiple), meningitis, and general weakness. One prisoner was shot while attempting to escape, another is suspected to have died of a gunshot to the head.[163]

Prof. Dr. Ziegler, who cared for prisoners as a chaplain and also kept death lists, reports that there were many deaths in 1942. In August, for example, a large number of deaths began, mainly among the Soviet prisoners. They mostly succumbed to dysentery, general exhaustion and tuberculosis. In 1944, the cases of typhus and tuberculosis increased. The causes of death of the Soviet soldiers can, therefore, mostly be traced back to poor nutrition, inadequate hygienic conditions and insufficient medical care.[164]

These findings are particularly dramatic when one considers that the Soviet prisoners in Moosburg were still treated comparatively well, since they had been brought to Reich territory quite specifically to perform forced labor, i.e., there was a certain interest in preserving their manpower. The situation in Moosburg, therefore, differed considerably from that in the camps for Soviet soldiers mainly in the east in the summer and autumn of 1941, where tens of thousands of captured Red Army soldiers died.[165] The situation in some of the camps in the Reich territory was also catastrophic. In Stalag XI C (Bergen-Belsen), 3,472 of the approximately 22,000 Soviet prisoners brought in by the end of 1941 died in January 1942 alone.[166]

The fact, that Italian prisoners were also treated relatively badly is shown by the fact that almost all the Italians who died had tuberculosis listed as the cause of death.[167]

Cremation of prisoners

The burial of prisoners was carried out according to completely different rules, depending on their

Figure 24: Cremation of Mahtab Singh according to Hindu rite

nationality. In a Stalag leaflet dated October 1, 1942, the procedures for funerals were precisely defined. Up to 30 members of the prisoner's work detachment were allowed to attend the funeral under adequate guard, but no civilians. In the case of British, French, and Yugoslav prisoners, the Wehrmacht provided an escort of honor. Pictures of these funeral ceremonies were to be taken; the OKW (Wehrmacht General Command) could then use the pictures for propaganda purposes. Special regulations applied to Polish and Soviet prisoners. There was no honorary delegation, no salute was fired and no wreath was laid by the Germans. Wreaths of prisoners were only allowed to have white or black ribbons, not in the national colors. For Soviet prisoners, it was further stipulated that burial was to be unobtrusive and in a simple form. Clergymen could participate if they belonged to the same POW camp. In the case of Muslims, "religious servants" were allowed to be called in if this was possible without special effort. The corpses of Muslims were to be buried with the head facing east and the face turned south (towards Mecca).[168]

According to other regulations, the burial of Soviet prisoners was to take place without clothing, insofar as this was still usable. Instead of coffins, the bodies had to be buried in paper covers or similar. As of March 1943, burial had to take place in tar, oil or asphalt paper.[169]

In the first years of the war, prisoners were buried in the nearest cemetery, as was the case in Moosburg. Those who died in the military hospital in Freising were buried in the St. Georg cemetery in Freising. When, after the arrival of the Soviet prisoners, the number of deaths skyrocketed, the Reich Ministry of the Interior decreed in October 1941 that the municipalities should bury Soviet prisoners in communal graves. The burial sites had to be in "remote locations," and ornamentation of the graves was forbidden.[170]

In accordance with this new regulation, those who died in the Stalag were buried in their own cemetery in Oberreit from autumn 1941 onwards, with sections for each nation. The prisoners buried in the Moosburg cemetery were moved to the cemetery in Oberreit. After the war, the cemetery in Oberreit was abandoned and the prisoners were reburied in central military cemeteries.[171]

In principle, burial in the ground was mandatory for the prisoners. However, there was also an exception in the Stalag: On December 1,1944, the British-Indian prisoner Mahtab Singh, died of tuberculosis in the camp hospital. In accordance with his wishes, he was cremated in a gravel pit north of the camp with an exceptional permit from the OKW, and his ashes were scattered in a stream.[172]

11. Sorting out of Soviet prisoners

Soviet prisoners were treated significantly worse than other groups of prisoners in many areas such as food, clothing equipment or medical care. They were largely without rights. The German government did not apply the Geneva Convention to them.[173] For Soviet soldiers, therefore, unlike prisoners from Western countries, captivity was a struggle for survival.

Sorting out in the POW camps 1941/1942

One of the greatest dangers, however, came from the so-called "Aussonderungen" (sorting out), especially in the autumn/winter of 1941/1942. This is the targeted killing of Soviet prisoners whom the German leadership considered "unacceptable" according to National Socialist ideology. This included "communist agitators",

"agitators", so-called "intelligentsia", the incurably ill and Jews.

The background to the separations was as follows. Before the attack on the Soviet Union, the Wehrmacht General Command (OKW) had issued the so-called "Kommissarbefehl" (commissar order), an order which stated that the political officers of the Soviet Army were to be executed while still on the battlefield. However, this order was not passed on to all units, nor was it followed everywhere. When the first Soviet prisoners arrived in Germany in the late summer of 1941 to perform forced labor, the German leadership feared that functionaries among the captured Soviet soldiers might be carrying out communist propaganda among the civilian population. This was the reason why the Gestapo received the order to search for "unacceptable" Soviet soldiers in the Stalags and the subcamps and to shoot them in the nearest concentration camp. It is estimated that about 38,000 Soviet prisoners fell victim to the Gestapo in this context.[174]

The sorting out in Stalag VII A

In Stalag VII A Moosburg, there is the only proven case of several Wehrmacht officers, namely members of the camp leadership and the Command of Military District VII, who jointly and systematically resisted the Gestapo.[175] The case has been the subject of historical research on several occasions[176] and is well documented. After the war, the Gestapo files were seized (they were used in the Nuremberg War Crimes Trials of the main war criminals).[177] In addition, there was an investigation against the Gestapo officials involved in 1950. Although this was without result, because some of the main persons responsible were already deceased and at the same time the investigation was conducted in a relatively superficial and lackadaisical manner, it

brought important insights into the course of events. In the investigation, the officers and Wehrmacht interpreters involved testified as witnesses.[178]

The Gestapo files, in particular, provide an unadulterated picture, since they were created directly during the events. The witness statements complement this picture, even if those involved sometimes confuse details and sequence of events that had already taken place eight years before. The statements of the Wehrmacht members appear reliable, since they largely correspond with each other and with the information from the Gestapo files.

These sources show that the Wehrmacht officers initially did not support the Gestapo's sorting-out operation and later downright sabotaged and thwarted it, although they were only successful to a limited extent. The confrontation between the Wehrmacht and the Gestapo proceeded, in simplified terms, in several phases and stages of escalation.

Phase 1: Camp administration and command of military district refuse to cooperate with the Gestapo.

In August 1941, the first Soviet prisoners arrived in Moosburg. On September 1, 1941, 4003 Red Army prisoners were registered in the area of Stalag VII A. On October 1, 1941, already 4916 Soviet soldiers were registered.[179] Most of these prisoners, many between the ages of 16 and their late 20s, were in the Stalag itself, where they were housed in a separate area, the "Russian camp".[180] In September 1941, an officer from the Munich Gestapo office asked the Command of Military District VII whether these prisoners had already been checked. The officers in charge answered in the affirmative, probably deliberately untruthfully.[181]

However, the Gestapo found out that this was not the case and asked for a personal consultation with the responsible officer at Command of Military District VII, Major Meinel[182]. Meinel declined and referred the matter to the commandant of Stalag VII A, Colonel Nepf, and the counterintelligence officer there, Captain Hörmann.[183] Colonel Nepf and Captain Hörmann, however, refused to cooperate with the Gestapo. They declined the request to make an administrative barrack available for interrogations and referred the officers to the "Russian camp," an affront in itself in view of the conditions prevailing there. Nor did Captain Hörmann divulge any information that would have made it easier for the Gestapo to sort out Soviet POW.[184] On September 29, the task force of five Gestapo officers began to check the camp on their own, with Wehrmacht interpreters translating on behalf of captain Hörmann[185]. Hörmann used the interpreters specifically to gain an insight into the activities of the Gestapo.[186]

Procedure of the reviews

The statements of the Wehrmacht interpreters allow us to understand how the segregation of the prisoners proceeded. The Gestapo had lists with the names of persons who were considered Soviet functionaries or members of the Soviet "intelligentsia." However, these lists were completely out of date and were partly based on false data. They were, therefore, useless. In order to be successful at all, the Gestapo commandos, therefore, had to proceed according to their own criteria. The officials apparently had little use for the term "intelligentsia" in particular. To be classified in this category, it was sufficient to have attended a ten-year school or to have worked as a postman, teacher, tailor or shoemaker! At the other hand, a few officials had to check thousands of prisoners in a short period of time. Thus, in Moosburg and its subcamps, 3088 prisoners were "interrogated" from September 29, 1941 to November 15 1941, up to 300 per day. In order to be able to cope with this large number at all, the officials took only a few minutes for the individual interrogations. They relied in part on informants, denunciation, and bribes of food and cigarettes. In some cases, physical force was used. The Wehrmacht interpreters sometimes had the impression that the only aim was to weed out as large a number of prisoners as possible.[187]

Of the 3088 prisoners checked, the Gestapo task force separated out 410 prisoners (among them 3 functionaries and officers, 25 Jews, 69 intelligentsia, 146 fanatical communists, 85 agitators and 47 incurably ill).[188] The Gestapo now asked Colonel Nepf to hand over these prisoners so that they could be transported in several groups to the Dachau Concentration Camp. Nepf and Hörmann had received instructions from the OKW on how to segregate the prisoners, but they had no information on what to do with them. They, therefore, first handed over those most concerning to the Gestapo, who took the prisoners to Dachau.[189]

Witness report of the shootings in Dachau

When the "Landesschützen" (guardsmen) guarding the first transport reported after their return that the prisoners had all been shot, Nepf and Hörmann had the next transport accompanied by a student assigned as interpreter in order to verify the Landesschützen's account.[190] After the end of the war, this student gave the following account of the events as a witness in the above-mentioned investigation:

"The prisoners were taken to a firing range with two firing lines.... Into one of these firing lines the trucks with

the Russian prisoners of war drove in backwards. The prisoners of war had to jump out of the truck and line up in a row of 5 people. Then the order was given that all the POW had to strip naked. ... The Russian prisoners of war realized at the moment when they had to undress what was to happen to them. The reaction to this was very different among them. A number carried out the order silently, and stood there paralyzed, others resisted, began to cry and scream... After a short time, the execution of the prisoners of war began. A group of 5 SS men each took a prisoner of war by the hand and led him at a run from one firing line into the other, in order to tie him to the wooden stakes about 1 m high in the front part of the firing line .... hereupon the SS men moved away and a group of, as far as I know, 20 armed SS men lined up at a distance of about 15m. At a command each of these SS men fired a shot. A large part of the 5 prisoners sank immediately but slowly to the ground. If one still remained standing, the leader of the command ran forward and shot the prisoner in question in the neck. Then the firing squad stepped aside and another group of SS men drove to the shot prisoners to load them onto a trolley. They then drove the corpses out of the firing range and threw them in a pile." [191]

Phase 2: The conflict with the Gestapo

Until then, the officers involved had merely not supported the Gestapo; now they began to take active action against the sorting out. This distinguishes them from most other Wehrmacht officers responsible for Soviet prisoners, who took no further interest in the fate of the segregated prisoners and simply took note of the fact that they were being executed. [192]

Colonel Nepf and Captain Hörmann now refused to assist the Gestapo in transporting the prisoners and refused to provide means of transport. Hörmann forbade the guards to report escape attempts or anything similar to the Gestapo. He also informed Major Meinel of the events. The latter called in his superior, Major General von Saur. [193]

Meinel and von Saur had already inspected the subcamps to learn how the Gestapo interrogated Soviet POW. They discovered that prisoners had also been mistreated by the Gestapo during interrogations. [194]

Meinel and Hörmann criticized the Gestapo for conducting their checks superficially, and, moreover, for shooting the prisoners in Dachau contrary to all international law. Major Meinel wrote a sharply worded protest. In it, he accused the task force of superficial job - a clever move, because the Gestapo officials were now attacked in their professional competence, and they came under pressure to justify themselves. Von Saur signed this protest and sent it to the highest-ranking German Wehrmacht officer responsible for prisoners of war, General Reinecke. He forwarded it to the Reich's Security Main Office (Reichssicherheitshauptamt, RSHA), the superior office of the Gestapo. [195] From there, the Munich Gestapo office was requested to carry out future sorting out strictly according to regulations and in agreement with the commandant of the prisoners of war in Military District VII. [196]

The Gestapo officials reacted aggrievedly. The procedure had been carried out strictly according to regulations; they said among other things, a form had been created for each prisoner. In addition, they complained about Meinel as someone who, to a certain extent, was averse to the National Socialist worldview. Furthermore, they tried to have Captain Hörmann replaced. [197]

Figure 25: Former SS shooting range in Hebertshausen, today a memorial site

Figure 26: Hebertshausen memorial on the former SS shooting range; plaques with the names of those who were shot

A discussion between the Gestapo and the officers of General Command VII to clarify the situation was fruitless. Von Saur referred to Meinel, who, however, insisted on his position and stated, among other things, that from the soldierly point of view the procedure was not to be approved of, since the prisoners would simply be shot. Moreover, the Soviet soldiers would be needed for labor. Finally, there was the added danger that the Soviet leadership would learn of these events and then treat German soldiers in the same way.[198]

Phase 3: Sabotage of the sorting out by the camp administration and the command of military district

By November 22, 1941, the Gestapo task force in Moosburg had separated out 455 prisoners. Of these, 267 had been taken to Dachau and murdered at the Hebertshausen firing range (today a memorial).[199]

Upon learning this, the officers involved refused to release the remaining 188 segregated prisoners.[200]

Initially, the Stalag simply ignored the request to hand over the prisoners to the Gestapo and transport them to Dachau. The camp administration forwarded a renewed request from the Gestapo to the command of military district VII in January 1942. Von Saur refused to extradite the prisoners, referring to the labor market situation, and demanded a new inspection.[201] The Gestapo office in Regensburg, which was responsible for the Lower Bavarian part of Military District VII, also learned that only 34 of the 278 segregated prisoners had been taken to Dachau. An official of the Gestapo office in Regensburg now negotiated the matter with Major Meinel but was also unsuccessful. He reported that he had gained the impression that Meinel was not only

interested in the workers themselves, but also in defying the Gestapo.[202]

In this context, an order by Hitler strengthened the position of the officers. In December 1941, the Führer had ordered that Soviet prisoners be increasingly used for work - an order that was at odds with the sorting out.[203]

Both sides were now looking for allies. Von Saur contacted the Bavarian State Labor Office and pointed out the importance of the Soviet prisoners for labor deployment. The State Labor Office, for its part, intervened with the RSHA. The Gestapo, in turn, turned to Gauleiter Wagner and received backing from there.[204]

The situation escalated further when it became known that on January 7, 1942, the segregated Soviet soldiers had been withdrawn from their previous work commands and distributed to newly-established work commands.[205] In this way, the Wehrmacht officers had deliberately and consciously sabotaged the activities of the Gestapo. Nepf, Hörmann, von Saur and Meinel had gone further in their resistance than other Wehrmacht officers responsible for Soviet prisoners.

The end of the conflict and the consequences for the officers involved

The Gestapo office in Munich now asked the RSHA to urge the OKW to hand over the prisoners.[206]

In February 1942, a compromise was reached between the OKW and the RSHA in Berlin: all sorted out prisoners in the camp were to be handed over to the Gestapo.

Prisoners on work detachments were to be checked a second time. The segregated prisoners were taken to Buchenwald Concentration Camp and re-examined by the Gestapo office in Weimar. Accordingly, one hundred twenty prisoners were not shot at that time, and some even have been alive to see the liberation of the concentration camp in April 1945.[207] Von Saur had also instructed Stalag VII A to provide a form for the Gestapo office in Weimar and the concentration camp in Buchenwald detailing the experiences with the prisoners during labor deployment, along with a short report on each individual prisoner by the respective labor command leader. He hoped that this would positively influence the decisions of the Gestapo officials.[208]

The consequences of the affair for the officers involved remained manageable. Colonel Nepf and Captain Hörmann remained at their posts, even though the latter received a kind of verbal reprimand from General Reinecke during an inspection visit to Moosburg.[209] Major General von Saur submitted his resignation, but was transferred to the Reserve on August 1, 1942, and subsequently promoted to Lieutenant General.[210] Major Meine became commander of a Stalag in Lithuania and a short time later was appointed Lieutenant Colonel.[211]

The motives of the officers

What motivated the four officers to initially not support the sorting out by the Gestapo, and later to deliberately sabotage it?

There are likely several different motives here. The argument that the prisoners were needed for work was probably a pretext, perhaps the only argument that the Gestapo would accept.

Initially, until it was verified that the extradited prisoners were murdered, the measure itself was probably less of an issue. The statements of some officers after the war suggest that they did not generally reject the segregation of prisoners who were considered

problematic. They initially understood this to mean the separation of this group from the other prisoners, not their murder.[212] At this stage they were probably more concerned with their pride as officers. Most of the officers involved were already 60 years of age or older.[213] That is, they had been trained in the military of the Imperial Era and had spent a considerable amount of time in service there. They considered it an affront and intolerable when civilians, in this case the Gestapo, made decisions over their area of responsibility on which they should have no influence. Thus, the interpreter quoted above reported that at the beginning of the inspections Captain Hörmann was annoyed that a foreign group wanted to interfere in the affairs of the Stalag.[214] Hörmann, for his part, spoke of the fact that Colonel Nepf stated to the General Command that cooperation with the Party or the Gestapo went against his military honor; he describes Nepf as an "anti-National-Socialist of the purest water."[215] This, then, had an effect when it was clear that the Soviet prisoners would be executed. It was against their code of honor as officers to shoot defenseless prisoners. Crucial at this stage, however, may have been the fear of what would happen to German prisoners in Soviet hands if the Soviet leadership learned of the shootings. This objection was also raised by Wehrmacht officers against the Commissar Order. Major Meinel also voiced this to the Gestapo.

In the end, however, the officers involved gave in. Von Saur and Meinel tried to protest to a higher level, even to the highest-ranking officer in the Wehrmacht for the prisoner-of-war service, but like Nepf and Hörmann they bowed to the pressure of their superiors. The fact that von Saur, Nepf, Meinel and Hörmann finally gave in to a large extent and obeyed an order that they recognized as unlawful is probably also due to their situation as veteran officers. For them, it was the utmost to raise objections to an order from superiors within the chain of command. To openly refuse an order, even one that was recognized as illegal, was simply inconceivable for these old-school officers. Their testimonies show that they did not even consider refusal a possibility.[216]

12. Escape and resistance

Escapes and escape attempts

A constant problem for the Stalags, the work commandos and the subcamps, were escapes and attempted escapes by prisoners. By August 1942, almost 78,000 prisoners had tried to escape throughout the Reich. Most of them could be recaptured, but the search for escaped prisoners meant a great effort for the military, the gendarmerie and the police.[217] During the war, detailed instructions were repeatedly issued to the various civil and military authorities on how to search for escaped prisoners and how the various authorities were to cooperate.[218]

In the course of the war, the number of attempted and successful escapes increased, partly because fewer and fewer guards were available. This affected the work detachments, in particular.[219] The commitment of civilians as additional auxiliary guards had no resounding success.[220]

The leadership of the German Reich considered escaped prisoners a considerable danger. On January 17, 1942, they ordered the establishment of the so-called "Landwacht." This was to protect the rural population from escaped prisoners, help to apprehend them and, thereby, relieve the police. A Landwacht post was then set up in the area of each gendarmerie post. The Landwacht guards were preferably recruited from the party, the SS and the SA. Their service was honorary, and

Figure 27: Escaped prisoner disguised as woman after his recapture

they were expected to provide their own weapons. No Landwacht was established in Moosburg. The mayor of Moosburg noted on the corresponding letter of February 9, 1942, that the establishment of a Landwacht for Moosburg was not necessary as Wehrmacht units were available for the prison camp.[221]

The Counterintelligence Group, headed by the counterintelligence officer, was responsible for preventing escape and sabotage. The latter had extensive authority to carry out his duties.[222] In the Stalag, the counterintelligence seems to have intensively researched escape plans, whether through

49

postal surveillance or informers. On July 7, 1942, for example, the camp administration informed the municipal construction office that one of the two prisoners employed there was thinking of escaping.[223]

The nights from Friday to Monday and over a holiday were particularly prone to escapes, as fewer guards were available. Colonel Burger, therefore, felt compelled to issue extensive instructions to the guard personnel in 1943. First, he urged increased vigilance on the days mentioned above. During the nights from Friday to Monday and over holidays, in addition to the normal guarding, extensive special measures were to be carried out: In all commands between 9 and 10 p.m., at least one count and identity roll call was conducted; between 11 p.m. and 5 a.m. at least one night inspection in all accommodation rooms, randomly. On Saturday afternoons, Sundays and holidays, outdoor patrols were also required. Supervisors should control the guard commands themselves during the night. The guards had to report important findings immediately to their superiors and to the Stalag, and cooperation with the police, other state agencies, and party offices "is a self-evident duty." In addition, great importance was attached to detailed and rapid escape reports.[224]

The guards were also allowed to shoot escaping prisoners, after appropriate threat. For Soviet soldiers, a warning was not mandatory.[225] However, the guards had to justify their behavior when shooting prisoners. Soldiers had to report to the gendarmerie and notify the division's court martial. The superior officer also had to take a stand. In addition, a coroner's inquest had to be held. Only when the court released the body, could it be buried.[226]

In the area of Stalag VII A there were 150-200 escape attempts per month, of which 10% succeeded. Of those, sixty to seventy percent of the escapees returned to the camp; the others, almost all Soviet soldiers, were taken to concentration camps by the criminal police. If they had committed crimes during their escape, for example stealing food, they had to be sent to a concentration camp.[227]

On a death list of the camp doctor for the years 1941-1944, it is noted that eight Soviet prisoners were "shot while trying to escape;" at least one American soldier was also shot while trying to escape. In the case of several other prisoners, the cause of death is also given as "gunshot wound" or "shot in the head," although it is unclear whether these were shootings during escape or for resistance.[228] The recapture of escaped prisoners and their punishment was to be announced on the notice board of the work detachments; The shooting of prisoners on the run was to be reported at roll call.[229]

Some escapes and escape attempts have been handed down in detail. A French priest who spoke German without an accent made three escape attempts. In the first, he took the passenger train from Munich to Augsburg, but was recognized by his commanding officer in the village of Kissing. On the third escape

Figure 28: Prison barrack in Stalag VII A

attempt, he tried to cross the border into Switzerland at Schaffhausen but ran in circles and ended up again in a German village instead of in the Swiss Confederation. He then voluntarily remained in the military hospital in Freising after the end of the war and was one of the last French prisoners to come home. Another French priest managed to escape by riding under a railroad car. One French prisoner was employed by a farmer at harvest time. With bicycle and scythe he rode from village to village as if he was just going to or coming from work. He also managed to escape.[230]

Punishment of prisoners

Civilians, i.e., also employers of prisoners, were not allowed to punish them. Disciplinary punishments were only allowed to be pronounced by the camp commandant, the leaders of a work commando, or their deputies. Imprisonment or the death penalty were imposed by the Wehrmacht courts.[231]

From Stalag VII A, an undated "Instruction Sheet for Disciplinary Punishment of POW" has been preserved. One of the principles was, "When judging whether a criminal act should be punished by the courts or by disciplinary action, the greatest leniency is to be exercised, especially in the case of criminal acts connected with an escape."[232] An escape, in itself, was not considered a criminal offense, but was only punished with arrest. In Moosburg, the "tariff" for escapes was one month's confinement in barrack 40, where the prisoner had to lie on the floor on straw.[233]

A whole range of possible punishment measures was forbidden: aggravation of working conditions, reduction in rank, corporal punishment "and any kind of cruelty at all." Restrictions on rations were permitted only to the extent that they could be imposed on German members of the Wehrmacht. Collective punishment for offenses committed by individuals was forbidden. If entire groups violated the rules, however, the camp authorities did impose collective punishments. A picture has survived showing numerous prisoners standing in a row at the camp fence, facing outwards, guarded by guards, while "standing for punishment."

Arrest was a permissible punitive measure, but its implementation was strictly regulated: The maximum duration, even for several offenses punished at the same time, was 30 days. Confinement in rooms that were not lit by daylight or were not hygienically maintained was forbidden. A break of three days was to be observed between the serving of two direct sentences. The prisoners had to be given the opportunity to exercise, clean themselves and spend at least two hours outdoors each day. Disciplined prisoners were allowed to read and write, receive and send letters. They had the right to present themselves at the daily medical examination. In order not to interfere too much with work duty, detention sentences had to be served on weekends as much as possible.

Double punishment was prohibited in a comprehensive sense. A judicial conviction precluded a disciplinary sentence, and a disciplinary sentence already served precluded the judicial conviction.

After serving their sentence, prisoners were not allowed to be treated differently from other prisoners. Only prisoners who had been punished for escape attempts could be supervised more strictly by the guards.[234]

Resistance

There are no records of camp uprisings or revolts from Stalag VII A. There were, however, cases of resistance by individual prisoners. The term "resistance" covers numerous different actions. These could be minor acts of rebellion and disobedience, refusal to work and sabotage during work assignments (increasingly from 1944 onwards), or even physical attacks on guards.[235] The guards were instructed to enforce obedience, for example the required work performance, with their weapon. As a last resort, they were also allowed to fire aimed shots at the prisoners. The Wehrmacht General Command (OKW) threatened the guards with severe punishment if they failed to force the prisoners to comply with their duty to work.[236]

Prisoners were also shot for resistance in the area of Stalag VII A. For example, on August 23, 1944, guards shot a British soldier on work duty in the village of Oberhummel "because of resistance and refusal to work." In the case of another, it seems likely that he was resisting or attempting to escape, as he died of a bullet to the head.[237] The guards tended to take the hardest line against resistance by Soviet prisoners. The camp doctor's list mentioned above lists "shot for mutiny" as the cause of death for three Soviet prisoners, and "shot for resistance" for one.[238]

However, there was also organized resistance. Time and again, prisoners, especially in the officers' camps, formed secret resistance movements. It was the task of the counterintelligence officer to identify resistance groups in the camp. He and his staff, therefore, tried to recruit informers among the prisoners.

Stalag VII A played a significant role in one of the most important underground organizations of Soviet prisoners in Germany, the B.S.W. ("Bratskoje Sotrudnitschestwo Wojennpleniich" = Fraternal Union of Prisoners of War). At the end of 1942/beginning of 1943, three Red Army soldiers in the "Schwanseestraße" work command in Munich founded the B.S.W. The group's program was ambitious: organizing and arming all prisoners of war and foreign workers in Germany,

overthrowing the Nazi regime by force, supporting the German workforce in an armed uprising against the National Socialists, providing assistance to the Red Army and the expected Western invasion forces, and committing acts of sabotage. The leaders of the organization initially expanded it within the camp. They trained members of the B.S.W. in sabotage and espionage, planned acts of sabotage and insurrection, procured weapons, and recruited for their organization among workers from Eastern Europe during the work detail. The B.S.W. was able to spread rapidly, as its members were often transferred to other cities. By the end of May 1943, there were already local committees in Karlsruhe, Heidelberg, Mannheim, Eppingen, Villingen, Baden-Baden, Ludwigsburg, Offenburg, Wiesenbach, and Rastatt. The B.S.W. was probably particularly successful in Munich. There, in the summer of 1943, B.S.W. agents were active in at least twelve Eastern workers' camps. In addition, the B.S.W. was able to establish contact with similar groups in Innsbruck, Vienna, and Prague, as well as with German Communists. In May 1943, the camp administration "Schwanseestraße" received indications of the existence of a secret organization among the prisoners. As a preventive measure, a large number of captured officers, among them the leading ones, were withdrawn and reassigned to Stalag VII A. Efforts were made in the Stalag to clarify the situation, but without success. Through skillful statements agreed upon in advance, the prisoners were able to largely disprove the suspicion of conspiracy. The camp authorities assigned the prisoners to a work detail in Dornach, where they resumed their activities for the B.S.W. and recruited new members. At the beginning of July 1943, 13 officers of the B.S.W. escaped in order to be able to develop activities outside the camp. They were soon apprehended and returned to the Moosburg camp, where they received 21 days of strict confinement. After serving this sentence, the prisoners were sent to the (punitive) work detachment No. 3370 Wildpoldsried, where they recruited fifty new members for the B.S.W. in a short time.

In the meantime, however, the Gestapo had come on the trail of the B.S.W. When the Gestapo realized its scope, it set up a special commission that uncovered the organization with the help of informers, among others. In the spring of 1944, the Gestapo arrested members of the B.S.W. throughout the Reich. Almost all of those arrested were sent to the Dachau concentration camp, where they were killed. In a report, the Munich Gestapo office noted that the organization, which "would certainly have assumed proportions dangerous to the German Reich in the near future," had been uncovered and 383 people arrested in the process. Then one could not refrain from taking a side swipe at the administration of Stalag VII A: "The highly treasonable enterprise of the Russian prisoners of war was promoted by the leadership of Stalag VII (A) in Moosburg - perhaps unconsciously - by the fact that the Russian prisoners of war suspected of Bolshevik activity, but especially the Jews and officers, were not handed over to the Gestapo in accordance with the decrees issued by the OKW, with the more detailed reasons being made known, but were distributed to other prisoner-of-war camps or work commandos."[239] This accusation was probably a tit-for-tat response to the heated conflict between the Gestapo office in Munich and the administration of Stalag VII A during the sorting out of Soviet prisoners in 1941/42.

However, this was not the only resistance group. Colonel Burger assumed that there were resistance groups in the camp that made secret contact with the Americans. However, he does not explain the scope of these groups and in what activities they were engaged. French prisoners in Stalag VII A allegedly joined together to form an organization close to the Resistance. The focus of this group is said to have been an attempt to establish contact with the advancing Americans. Whether, and to what extent, this succeeded is uncertain.[240]

13. Liberation of the camp and end of the war in Moosburg on April 29, 1945

The situation in the Reich

In the last days of April, the situation of the German troops in Bavaria as well as in the Reich was hopeless. Shrunken and inadequately equipped units faced an Allied superiority overwhelming in men and material, which meanwhile also had unrestricted air supremacy.

On October 21, 1944, the American forces were able to conquer Aachen, the first major German city. In January 1945, the Red Army had reached the Oder, and on March 7 the US Army had crossed the Rhine. The defense in the west had collapsed, one city after another, along the Rhine was occupied by Americans and British. After American units had reached the Elbe River near Magdeburg on April 11, American and Soviet troops met at Torgau on April 25; the Western Front had united with the Eastern Front. The area, still controlled by the Germans, had, thus, been divided into north and south. When the Soviet forces had closed their ring around Berlin on April 25, the battle for the Reich capital began. On April 29, house-to-house fighting raged in Berlin. Hitler married Eva Braun in the embattled Reich Chancellery and dictated his political and personal testament.[241]

The situation in Bavaria

Bavaria, too, had long been a combat zone by the end of April 1945. After conquering the Rhine plain, American troops had advanced south and east along the Rhine and Main rivers. On March 25, 1945, American forces had entered Bavarian soil near Aschaffenburg and had since occupied Bavaria from north to south. French troops were operating in Swabia. After conquering Franconia, the 7th U.S. Army under General Alexander McCarrell Patch crossed the Danube at Dillingen on April 22, reaching the area of Military District VII. The 7th U.S. Army then began conquering the western parts of southern Bavaria, while the 3rd U.S. Army under General George S. Patton essentially took over the occupation of southeastern Bavaria.[242] On April 26, American troops entered Ulm, and on April 27, Regensburg and Ingolstadt were taken.[243]

The American forces advanced rapidly in Bavaria as well. They were able to quickly bypass pockets of German resistance or crush them with superior air power. According to some historians, the Bavarian country roads, clogged with refugees, members of evacuated offices and scattered soldiers, represented a greater obstacle to the American advance than the German troops.[244]

In this situation, chaotic structures of power prevailed in many places in Bavaria. The offices of the Wehrmacht were overwhelmed by the situation and difficult to reach because of the frequent changes of position; effective military leadership was almost non-existent. State and municipal authorities, offices of the Reich that had been transferred to the south, party organizations and groups such as the Hitler Youth and the Gauleiter, police leaders, the "Volkssturm" (militia raised at the end of the war), and various SS units exercised power together or against each other and organized "defense measures".[245] In this tangle of confusing power structures, often exacerbated by the rapid collapse of the German lines of defense, leeway repeatedly opened up for individual officials and officers to make independent and far-reaching decisions. However, there was always the danger of summary execution if another commander or holder of power judged an order to be treason or cowardice in the face of the enemy.

The situation in Moosburg

There are several eyewitness accounts of the last days of the war and the first days of peace, which illuminate the events from different perspectives. Camp Commandant, Colonel Otto Burger, describes the events during the last days of April, August Alckens, interpreter in the camp at the time, reports above all on the situation in the barracks of the guards during the liberation of the camp. Major Rudolf Koller, commander of the Landes-schützen battalion 512 (guards of the Stalag) and Combat Commander of Moosburg, describes the military procedures and the invasion of the US troops in Moosburg. Finally, the parish priest, Alois Schiml, describes the last phase of the war in Moosburg and the situation of the civilian population in the town during and after the invasion of the Americans. Although not all the details are the same as far as the course of events and the time specifications are concerned, the synopsis provides a relatively-detailed picture of the events.

In the spring of 1945, the end of the war also became apparent in Moosburg and the surrounding area. The fact that the fronts were moving closer had become obvious when several military hospitals were transferred from Silesia to Freising during the last months of the war.[246]

Especially in April, the bombing raids on Erding, Freising and Landshut caused more and more frequent air raid alarms in Moosburg. There were four air-raid shelters in the town, including one at the fire station on the Moosburg central square (now the town library), and some Moosburg residents had also dug slit trenches in their gardens.[247]

The fact that the war had now also reached the Moosburg area was clearly demonstrated to the population by numerous low-flying air raids. Because of the straight route, the railway line and the road between the villages of Langenbach and Marzling were particularly popular targets for the American pilots. In addition, there was a low-flying attack on a passenger train near Isareck close to Moosburg which left 18 dead. On March 24, bombs, presumably an emergency drop from a damaged American fighter plane, fell on an open field near the bridge over the river Amper and killed a farmer.[248]

In the last days of April, the situation worsened. Refugees poured into the town, the thunder of cannons could already be heard. On April 26, long columns of concentration camp prisoners crossed the town in "pitiful condition," as Koller writes. Nine of them died in Thonstetten, a village close to Moosburg. Liberated by US troops, the concentration camp prisoners returned to Moosburg immediately after the end of the war and were supplied with Red Cross parcels.[249]

In addition, at the end of April long military convoys drove through from Landshut in the direction of Munich; on one day, among others, eleven generals with their staffs passed Moosburg with the destination Garmisch. When the traffic slowed down, this was the sign for Major Koller that the front was now in the immediate vicinity.[250]

Figure 29: Complete overcrowding in the last days before liberation: prisoners camped between barracks in the open air

The situation in the Stalag

The end of the war also made its mark in the Stalag. The German leadership had prisoner-of-war camps evacuated, especially before the collapsing Eastern Front, so that no prisoners would fall into the hands of the enemy. Therefore, since the end of 1944, thousands of prisoners came to Moosburg. Among them, were about 12,000 officers, for example 2,000 Air Force officers from Stalag Luft III (Sagan in Silesia) as well as the entire Eichstätt officers' camp. Because rail transport had partially collapsed, they often had to march long distances with insufficient supplies and understandably arrived at the Stalag exhausted and often sick.[251]

The figures given as to how many prisoners were in the camp at the end of the war vary: Major Koller gives a figure of 33,000[252], the Red Cross 37,000[253], Colonel Burger both 60,000 and 70,000[254], Prof. Dr. Ziegler 70,000[255], an edition of the American army newspaper Army Times 130,000[256], although the latter probably includes not only prisoners from the main camp but also from satellite camps. The number of about 70,000 might be realistic for the following reasons: As of December 1, 1944, there were 75,400 prisoners in the Stalag area, 56,350 of whom were on work duty. According to the last occupancy report for Stalag VII A, on January 1, 1945, there were approximately 76,000 prisoners in the area of the Stalag, i.e., in the camp itself and in the subcamps.[257] This means that even before a large number of additional prisoners arrived in the Stalag because of the evacuations, there were already about 20,000 inmates there. In order to be able to accommodate the new arrivals, the camp administration requisitioned tents for 30,000 people.[258] Contemporary witnesses also report that the camp was completely overcrowded, which is confirmed by pictures showing numerous prisoners crowding between barracks in the camp area, where they obviously had to camp out in the open.[259] If one considers that even in 1943/44 there were up to 20,000 prisoners in the camp,[260] that the occupancy density in the barracks had been significantly increased since the end of 1944,[261] that the camp administration still had tents erected for 30,000 prisoners in the open areas, such as the sports field, and that prisoners, nevertheless, had to spend the night in the open, then such oppressive occupancy can only have been caused by a population of 70,000 prisoners.

In times of an increasingly chaotic situation, the camp administration had to supply an ever-increasing number of people. Since it was difficult to bring supplies into the Stalag due to the widespread destruction of the transport infrastructure and the low-flying air raids, the food parcels from the Red Cross were particularly important. In March, the Red Cross had taken up quarters in Moosburg and from there distributed food parcels, which had been delivered by several trains, to various camps by truck.[262]

At the same time, the camp administration tried to prevent the Gestapo or the SS from gaining access to the camp and to maintain peace in the camp. The camp administration had 2000 guards at its disposal for the camp and another 8000 guards for the 80,000 prisoners in subcamps.[263]

The command situation

At the end of April, Colonel Burger had received orders to march south with the captured officers. They were probably to serve as a bargaining chip in possible negotiations with the Allies. Such a march without prepared food and lodging would have meant considerable hardships and for some of the prisoners death. The troops were to remain in Moosburg, but the camp buildings were to be blown up so as not to let any accommodation fall into the hands of the enemy. All soldiers not directly needed for guarding had to be incorporated into the fighting force. A defense line was to be established along the Isar and Amper rivers.[264]

In this situation, Colonel Burger, Major Koller and, allegedly, also Mayor Müller decided to surrender the town and the camp without a fight and without removing prisoners. Major Koller was already making arrangements to guard the depots with the Red Cross parcels and other camps to avoid looting.[265] It was especially important to prevent the destruction of the bridge over the river Isar. On April 24, in fact, the command of Military District VII had ordered that the Isar bridges be prepared for "lasting destruction".[266] In fact, engineer officers arrived in Moosburg to attach explosive charges to the Isar Bridge. Otherwise, the troops in Moosburg did not receive any concrete orders; the military leadership was left to its own devices and was hardly able to contact the superior authorities.[267]

Now leeway to act opened up for the players in Moosburg.

Apr 27, 1945

On April 27, 1945, at 8:30 p.m., the Commander in Chief West issued an order to prepare, among other things, a defense line Isar-Amper-Glonn-Ammersee-Schongau as a rearward bar.[268] The defense order, also valid for Moosburg, read: *"The hour of decision has come. It is a matter of last resistance and victory. The Isar-Amper-Glonn line is the last defensive position. It must be held. From here, the great offensive begins. New, best-equipped divisions are ready. Decisive weapons, hitherto unknown, are being brought to bear."* Mutineers and deserters were to be ruthlessly dealt with, and everyone had the duty to remove failing officers in order to take the lead themselves.[269]

Moosburg was located in the operational area of the 1st German Army. This consisted of a hodgepodge of remnant units of the Wehrmacht, the Waffen-SS and the Volkssturm.[270] The commander of Military District VII had three divisions to secure his defense area. One of them, which was to defend a section of 14 km, consisted of a colonel as division commander, his driver and his ordonnance. The division commander was to replenish his unit with soldiers who were flooding back.[271]

Colonel Burger tried to convince the command of the military district to declare the area around Moosburg a neutral territory in which no fighting should take place. The command of the military district was not averse to this proposal, but before a decision was made, the defensive section around Moosburg was placed under the XIII SS Army Corps (consisting of the 38th SS Panzer Grenadier Division "Nibelungen" and the 352nd Volksgrenadier Division). The SS Division "Nibelungen" was to defend the area around Moosburg with three regiments. It was joined by parts of the SS Division "Charlemagne".[272]

Apr 28, 1945

On April 28,1945, the first SS units arrived in Moosburg. A regiment of the "Nibelungen" division took up position in the town. The SS commander responsible for Moosburg was determined to defend Moosburg with his troops and the guards of the Stalag "in the most sustainable way".[273]

According to Colonel Burger, the news of the "Freiheitsaktion Bayern" (movement for a free bavaria), an attempted uprising by some Wehrmacht units in the Munich area against the National Socialist rulers with the goal of ending the war, initially triggered elation on April 28, 1945, which was followed by disillusionment after the suppression of the uprising was announced. The "Freiheitsaktion Bayern" also had contact with a resistance group consisting of interpreters in Stalag VII A and other groups in the Freising area.[274]

On the morning of the same day, Colonel Burger announced to the Stalag personnel and the guard force that the prisoners would not be removed, Moosburg would not be defended, and the guard force would not be incorporated into the combat force. He wanted to hand the camp over to the Americans. He then explained this to the prisoners. Thus, Colonel Burger had refused an order in public. Against the background of the general command situation, he and the men supporting him put their lives in danger.

Colonel Burger and Major Koller began to prepare for the surrender of the town and camp without a fight. Major Koller, as in previous days, instructed the commanders of the Moosburg Volkssturm to maintain peace and order, to avoid looting and above all any bloodshed, and to protect the prisoners. They were not, however, to make any preparations for hostilities.[275] There are reports that Moosburg citizens also began to hide bazookas or render them useless, and some attempted to remove explosive charges from the Amper Bridge at night.[276]

When it became known around noon that the towns of Mainburg and Nandlstadt were already occupied, and scouts reported that U.S. troops (the 14th Armored Division of the Third U.S. Army) had reached the village of Mauern the authorities in the camp and in Moosburg had to act. Colonel Burger decided to contact the American commander and inform him of his intentions. Representatives of the Red Cross and the most senior American and British officers were to leave for Mauern at about 2 p.m. as a negotiating delegation and enter into talks with the Americans. The top priority was to dissuade the SS from defending Moosburg or to induce them to withdraw. At first, Colonel Burger did not succeed in persuading the SS commanders not to obey their orders. He pointed out to the SS commander that there could be considerable consequences if prisoners of war were killed in combat under the eyes of the Red Cross. The SS officer should, instead, negotiate a neutral zone without fighting with the Americans. Then he would not be breaking any orders, since he would not have to fight if he was not attacked. Thereupon, the SS leader decided to follow Colonel Burger's plan and to agree with the Americans to leave Moosburg out of the eventual fighting. At about 3:30 p.m., the delegation left with the SS officer for the front.[277] According to the information given by Colonel Burger, the SS officer was held by the US troops. Whether this was actually the case is not entirely clear. The negotiating delegation returned at 6 p.m. and announced that the Americans had promised to treat the Stalag personnel according to international law and to release them from captivity

soon. No reprisals, looting or rioting would be permitted in Moosburg. However, the agreement on a neutral zone was rejected, and the German troops were ordered to surrender.[278]

The background for the behavior of the US commanders might have been that they feared that the SS might retreat in an orderly fashion across the Isar Bridge, taking prisoners with them and blowing up the Isar Bridge.

It was expected that the American troops would arrive in Moosburg around noon on April 29. Still on April 28, Colonel Burger discussed with captured officers the handing over of the camp, especially the rations, the hospital, the card index, the deposited valuables of the prisoners and five million Reichsmark in foreign currency. In the evening, American and British officers were sent to the individual units and also to the battalion staff of the Landesschützen stationed in Moosburg to coordinate and supervise the measures discussed.[279]

The night from April 28 to 29,1945

During the night of April 28-29, a large part of the SS gradually withdrew from the area around Moosburg. Colonel Burger states that he pretended to the then leaderless SS that they had received orders to clear the area around Moosburg.[280] This is not comprehensible. Even if Colonel Burger's account that the Americans had captured the SS commander sent as a parliamentary is correct, the SS in Moosburg could still have contacted the division command post or another regiment and clarified the situation with the officers there. It is more likely that the SS retreated before the overwhelming superiority of the US troops.[281]

The retreating SS units prepared the Isar Bridge for blowing up. Major Koller lobbied hard for the bridge not to be blown up, pointing out its great importance for the supply of Upper Bavaria. At first, he was successful, the SS leaders promised to spare the bridge.[282]

During the night of April 28-29, the camp authorities withdrew the guards from the interior of the camp, and the prisoners now took over the security measures themselves. Allied soldiers were assigned to all German posts on the outer guard towers. Major Koller, together with an American and a British officer, inspected the various depots in Moosburg in preparation for the approaching surrender.[283]

Apr 29, 1945 - The conquest of Moosburg

In the early morning hours of April 29, parts of an SS unit began to entrench themselves on the heights near the village of Ziegelberg and at the Amper river at the gates of Moosburg. An SS officer ordered the Moosburg "Volkssturm" (militia) to dig foxholes there. By this time, most of the Volkssturm men had already retreated. Major Koller asked the Volkssturm commander to send some Volkssturm men to the Amper river with pickaxes and shovels as a pretense.[284]

Around nine o'clock, rifle fire and German machine gun fire could be heard from the direction of Wittibsmühle close to the Amper river. The entrenched SS units began to resist the US troops advancing from the village of Mauern north of Moosburg. A battle developed around the bridge across the river, and the Americans' advance was initially disrupted. Around 10 o'clock, coming from the west, American tanks approached the town. Soon, 15-20 US tanks were on the heights of the Amper river and took the area around the Amper Bridge under fire.

Out of consideration for the prisoners, the Americans did not use heavy artillery, in contrast to their usual approach to resistance. However, a few shells hit Moosburg, and the church tower was also shelled. By that time, the people of Moosburg had prematurely ended Sunday services and retreated to their cellars.

The American tanks were approaching the Amper Bridge. Since the SS troops did not have any heavy weapons such as anti-tank guns, and bazookas had been rendered useless in Moosburg, the American tanks were able to quickly break the SS resistance.

Around 11 a.m., the SS retreated fighting across the Amper River to Moosburg, pursued by American troops, and entrenched themselves in the town. The Americans followed and entered Moosburg. SS members had also set up a position in the tower of Moosburg's St John's Church and fired from there at the advancing US troops. Brief but fierce firefights ensued in the streets of the town. American tanks, coming from the Amper Bridge, quickly drove past St. Kastulus Church in the direction of the Isar Bridge in order to occupy it as quickly as possible and thus forestall its destruction. Before they could reach the bridge, however, it was blown up by the retreating SS. In a short time, American infantry occupied the town. The US soldiers searched the houses for weapons, hidden soldiers and cameras. Tanks gathered on Moosburg's main streets. The GIs were greeted by the people of Moosburg with flowers; most of the people of Moosburg had already flown white flags. Nothing is known about casualties among the civilian population. Some houses and also the tower of St. John's Church showed minor bullet holes.[285]

The liberation of Stalag VII A

Only now, after the capture of the city, did the US troops turn their attention to the camp. The main goal of the

American commanders was probably to capture the Isar Bridge, undestroyed, and, thus, secure an intact crossing over the river, as well as to disrupt the retreat of the German troops. The Americans, therefore, concentrated first on the town, and only later on the camp.[286]

When the first American tanks were sighted approaching the Stalag from the field, the Allied prisoners took over the posts on the watchtowers and by then were guarding the camp. The prisoners were already awaiting the arrival of the liberators when the battle between SS and US troops broke out. At 11:30 a.m., shells hit the ante-camp, directed against the SS positions on the railroad embankment near the camp, injuring several Germans. Many prisoners now retreated to hastily-dug slit trenches. About noon, the first American tanks arrived at the camp, headed by the division commander. Colonel Burger handed over the camp to him. The handover lasted only a few minutes. The work detachments, which had also received orders to this effect, surrendered to the American troops without a fight.[287] The Stalag VII A was history.

Of particular interest is a paragraph at the end of Colonel Burger's report. Even before certifying that his officers and men had acted conscientiously, he expressed his "highest respect" for the prisoners for their conduct, which had made it possible to keep the SS and others in the dark about his plans and to surrender the camp without a fight as planned. Thus, in the last days of the war, the fronts had changed. No longer were there German troops and authorities against the prisoners of war, but parts of the German troops and prisoners of war against the SS and Gestapo.[288]

For the guards, the war was also over, albeit not until early afternoon. While the fighting for Moosburg was still going on after noon, the German soldiers received

Figure 30: American soldiers drive their tanks through the camp area

three days' worth of marching rations and their military pay in the barracks of the guards. Meanwhile, the officers ate roast goose and pork in the canteen. At about 2:30 p.m., American troops occupied the barracks of the guards and disarmed the Landesschützen.[289]

German soldiers, as well as civilians such as Mayor Müller and the entire town council, were gathered at a large square of Moosburg and, like the Landesschützen

Figure 31: The liberation of the camp

and Stalag personnel, were led north into captivity in the late afternoon.[290]

The first hours and days of the post-war period

In the following days, the population of Moosburg had to experience sometimes violent attacks by American soldiers and former prisoners of war.

The invading Americans took wedding rings and watches from the civilian population of Moosburg. US soldiers also took up quarters in private houses. Their inhabitants usually had only one hour to pack the most necessary things and to look for a substitute accommodation.[291]

Already in the afternoon of April 29, 1945 there was extensive looting. Groups of prisoners from the camp streamed into the town. They looted shops, farms and private houses. Parish priest Schiml writes that the buildings were searched from cellar to attic, food, blankets, beds but also preserving jars and frying pans were taken. Much of what the prisoners could not use, they destroyed.

The Wehrmacht had stored 8,000 liters of wine in a cellar, which former prisoners of war consumed. The next day, the military government ordered 40 coffins for those prisoners who had succumbed to alcohol. After a few days, the Americans closed the cellar. Angry prisoners set fire to it as well as to the property of a farmer who had hesitated to surrender a calf. A military shoe store at the train station was cleared out, during which locals also participated. The local museum and a school building were also looted, in the latter mainly maps. Prisoners returned to the Stalag with clothing, food and all sorts of other items.[292]

There were also some cases of rapes, committed by prisoners of war. It was particularly problematic that lists containing the names of all residents and their ages had to be posted on the houses. When it became known on the second day of the looting that there had already been 17 rapes, the town priest and chaplains set up shelters for women and girls in the rectory of St. Kastulus and in the chaplain's houses.[293]

Although the U.S. troops tried to prevent attacks, contain looting and return looted objects, they were overwhelmed by the chaotic situation. This situation was further aggravated when, over time, prisoners of war and civilian internees housed in the surrounding area also flocked to Moosburg. At the same time, however, many former prisoners tried to prevent attacks, especially on families and businesses where they had been treated well during their work assignments. There are numerous reports that former prisoners set up posts in front of the relevant buildings and even used violence to protect Moosburg citizens.

After eight days, the Americans were able to contain the looting to a large extent with massive efforts, but this was only completely achieved after 14 days, as new looters from the surrounding area kept coming.[294]

Prof. Dr. Ziegler, who visited Moosburg on May 3, 1945, confirms Father Schiml's report. According to his recollections, the town was deserted, no Germans were to be seen on the streets, only foreigners. Standing in front of the parsonage, a heap of misery, completely distraught, Father Schiml reported that many women had been raped during the capture of the town. There were still sick Germans in the camp hospital, and it was like a beehive in the camp.[295]

In these days after liberation, Moosburg received a visit from a high-ranking officer. General Patton, Commander of the Third Army, came to the camp with his staff. Reports have survived from American soldiers who were impressed by his appearance. Allegedly, Patton had himself driven down the main camp road standing on a tank, brandishing his famous ivory-tipped Colts.

It was one of his last public appearances during the Second World War. Even for the part of Bavaria that was not yet occupied, the war lasted only a few more days. On the evening of April 29, the Americans conquered the town of Freising, and on April 30, Munich. On May 4, the entire area of Military District VII was occupied by American and French troops. On May 6, at 12:00 p.m., the surrender of the German troops in the southern area, which also included Bavaria, came into effect. Even though it was difficult to reach all units in view of the chaotic conditions, the Second World War was over in Bavaria, and two days later in the whole of Europe.[296]

Endnotes

[1] Transcript of a lecture given by Colonel Nepf to citizens of Moosburg in the Stalag canteen in January 1941, Moosburg Municipal Archives, 06/45, p. 1.

[2] Otto R., Wehrmacht, Gestapo und sowjetische Gefangene im deutschen Reichsgebiet 1941/42, Munich 1998, p. 27ff; Speckner H., In der Gewalt des Feindes, Vienna 2003, p. 19ff.

[3] Otto R., Wehrmacht, Gestapo und sowjetische Gefangene im deutschen Reichsgebiet 1941/42, Munich 1998, p. 29 FN 14.

[4] Otto R., Wehrmacht, Gestapo und sowjetische Gefangene im deutschen Reichsgebiet 1941/42, Munich 1998, p. 29; Pfahlmann H., Fremdarbeiter und Kriegsgefangene in der deutschen Kriegswirtschaft 1939-1945, Darmstadt 1968, pp. 83ff.

[5] Federal Military Archives, RHD 4, 138/12.

[6] Transcript of a lecture given by Colonel Nepf to citizens of Moosburg in the Stalag canteen in January 1941, Moosburg Municipal Archives, 06/45, p. 1.

[7] Memorandum of the mayor of Moosburg, Dr. Müller, "Kriegsgefangenenlager in Moosburg" from 19.09.1939 to 21.09.1939, Moosburg Municipal Archives, 06/47; Federal Military Archives, RH 53-7/v. 724, p. 12f.

[8] Nowak E., Polnische Kriegsgefangene im Dritten Reich, in: Bischof G./Karner S./Stelzl-Marx B. (eds.), Kriegsgefangene des Zweiten Weltkriegs, Vienna 2005, pp. 507-517, p. 508, especially with reference to Polish research; Bedürftig F., Drittes Reich und Zweiter Weltkrieg, Munich 2004, "Polenfeldzug".

[9] Otto R., Wehrmacht, Gestapo und sowjetische Gefangene im deutschen Reichsgebiet 1941/42, Munich 1998, p. 29.

[10] Otto R., Wehrmacht, Gestapo und sowjetische Gefangene im deutschen Reichsgebiet 1941/42, Munich 1998, p. 30.

[11] Federal Military Archives, RHD 4, 138/12.

[12] Federal Military Archives, RHD 4, 138/12.

[13] Otto R., Wehrmacht, Gestapo und sowjetische Gefangene im deutschen Reichsgebiet 1941/42, Munich 1998, p. 29.

[14] Transcript of a lecture given by Colonel Nepf to citizens of Moosburg in the Stalag canteen in January 1941, Moosburg Municipal Archives, 06/45, p. 1.

[15] Report by a member of the Reich Labor Service, „Erinnerungen eines `Arbeitsmannes` an den Beginn von Stalag VII, September 1939", Moosburg Municipal Archives, Bestand Stalag VII A Berichte Beginn-Ende, pp. 2ff.

[16] Otto R., Wehrmacht, Gestapo und sowjetische Gefangene im deutschen Reichsgebiet 1941/42, Munich 1998, p. 30.

[17] Nowak E., Polnische Kriegsgefangene im Dritten Reich, in: Bischof G./Karner S./Stelzl-Marx B. (eds.), Kriegsgefangene des Zweiten Weltkriegs, Vienna 2005, pp. 507-517, pp. 515f.

[18] Report by a member of the Reich Labor Service, "Erinnerungen eines `Arbeitsmannes' an den Beginn von Stalag VII, September 1939," Moosburg Municipal Archives, Bestand Stalag VII A Berichte Beginn-Ende, p. 3; transcript of a lecture by Colonel Nepf, to Moosburg citizens in the Stalag canteen in January 1941, Moosburg Municipal Archives, 06/45, p. 2.

[19] Report by a member of the Reich Labor Service, „Erinnerungen eines `Arbeitsmannes` an den Beginn von Stalag VII, September 1939", Moosburg Municipal Archives, Bestand Stalag VII A Berichte Beginn-Ende, p. 3.

[20] Transcript of a lecture given by Colonel Nepf to citizens of Moosburg in the Stalag canteen in January 1941, Moosburg Municipal Archives, 06/45, p. 2f.

[21] Otto R., Wehrmacht, Gestapo und sowjetische Gefangene im deutschen Reichsgebiet 1941/42, Munich 1998, p. 31 FN 26.

[22] Otto R., Wehrmacht, Gestapo und sowjetische Gefangene im deutschen Reichsgebiet 1941/42, Munich 1998, p. 30 FN 20.

[23] Transcript of a lecture given by Colonel Nepf to citizens of Moosburg in the Stalag canteen in January 1941, Moosburg Municipal Archives, 06/45, p. 2.

[24] Minutes of 17.11.1939, Moosburg Municipal Archives, 06/47.

[25] Thus, in a letter dated 14 May 1941, the town administration asked the Graf von Preysing'sche Güterverwaltung whether it would be willing to sell land to Moosburg farmers who had to cede land for the construction of the Stalag. The inquiry remained without result. Moosburg Municipal Archives, 06/47.

Endnotes

[26] Memorandum by Mayor Dr. Müller „Gefangenenlager in Moosburg betreffend" dated 21.09.1939, Moosburg Municipal Archives, 06/47

[27] Report by a member of the Reich Labor Service, „Erinnerungen eines `Arbeitsmannes` an den Beginn von Stalag VII, September 1939". Moosburg Municipal Archives, Bestand Stalag VII A Berichte Beginn-Ende, p. 4.

[28] Transcript of a lecture given by Colonel Nepf to citizens of Moosburg in the Stalag canteen in January 1941, Moosburg Municipal Archives, 06/45, p. 7.

[29] Otto R., Wehrmacht, Gestapo und sowjetische Gefangene im deutschen Reichsgebiet 1941/42, Munich 1998, p. 32.

[30] Otto R., Wehrmacht, Gestapo und sowjetische Gefangene im deutschen Reichsgebiet 1941/42, Munich 1998, p. 32.

[31] Otto R., Wehrmacht, Gestapo und sowjetische Gefangene im deutschen Reichsgebiet 1941/42, Munich 1998, p. 28.

[32] Transcript of a lecture given by Colonel Nepf to citizens of Moosburg in the Stalag canteen in January 1941, Moosburg Municipal Archives, 06/45, p. 2.

[33] Otto R., Wehrmacht, Gestapo und sowjetische Gefangene im deutschen Reichsgebiet 1941/42, Munich 1998, p. 32, FN 30; Speckner H., In der Gewalt des Feindes, Vienna 2003, p. 38ff.

[34] Keller M., Was ist geschehn?, Moosburg 1995, p. 57.

[35] Nowak E., Polnische Kriegsgefangene im Dritten Reich, in: Bischof G./Karner S./Stelzl-Marx B. (eds.), Kriegsgefangene des Zweiten Weltkriegs, Vienna 2005, pp. 507-517, p. 515f; Spoerer M., Zwangsarbeit unter dem Hakenkreuz, Munich 2001, p. 101.

[36] Cf. a list of forbidden items, compiled by POW Camp VII A, Gruppe III, Federal Military Archives, RH 49/49, p. 63.

[37] Detailed report in the transcript of a lecture by Colonel Nepf, to citizens of Moosburg in the Stalag canteen in January 1941, Moosburg Municipal Archives, 06/45, p. 3f.

[38] Transcript of a lecture given by Colonel Nepf to citizens of Moosburg in the Stalag canteen in January 1941, Moosburg Municipal Archives, 06/45, p. 4.

[39] Matiello G., Prisoners of War in Germany 1939-1945, Lodi 2003, p. 76.

[40] Memorandum by Mayor Dr. Müller „Gefangenenlager in Moosburg betreffend" dated 21.09.1939, Moosburg Municipal Archives, 06/47.

[41] For example, 20 prisoners had been employed in road construction since mid-November; a contract to this effect between the town and the Stalag dates from 15 November 1939, Moosburg Municipal Archives, 06/57. In addition, numerous prisoners were employed in the construction of the town's main canal in the summer and autumn of 1940, Municipal Archives of Moosburg, 06/31.

[42] POW Camp VII, Gruppe III, „Brief- und Paketpost", Federal Military Archives RH 49/49 p. 33.

[43] Ziegler A., Ein Werk des Friedens, Munich 1979, pp. 130f., 174.

[44] Speckner H., In der Gewalt des Feindes, Vienna 2003, p. 81f.

[45] POW Camp VII, Gruppe III, "Brief und Paketpost", Federal Military Archives, RH 49/49, p. 33.

[46] Speckner H., In der Gewalt des Feindes, Vienna 2003, p. 73, with reference to a leaflet of the OKW of 20.07.1942.

[47] POW Camp VII, Gruppe III, „Brief- und Paketpost", Federal Military Archives, RH 49/49, p. 33; Speckner H., In der Gewalt des Feindes, Vienna 2003, p. 73.

[48] POW Camp VII, Gruppe III, „Brief- und Paketpost", Federal Military Archives, RH 49/49, p. 33b; Speckner H., In der Gewalt des Feindes, Vienna 2003, pp. 74ff.

[49] Transcript of a lecture given by Colonel Nepf to citizens of Moosburg in the Stalag canteen in January 1941, Moosburg Municipal Archives, 06/45, p. 9.

[50] Speckner H., In der Gewalt des Feindes, Vienna 2003, p. 72ff.

[51] Speckner H., In der Gewalt des Feindes, Vienna 2003, p. 72, p. 72 FN 155 with reference to a leaflet of the OKW of 20.07.1942.

[52] Speckner H., In der Gewalt des Feindes, Vienna 2003, p. 81ff; Ziegler A., In der Gewalt des Feindes, Munich 1979, p. 133.

[53] Transcript of a lecture given by Colonel Nepf to citizens of Moosburg in the Stalag canteen in January 1941, Moosburg Municipal Archives, 06/45, p. 9.

[54] Speckner H., In der Gewalt des Feindes, Vienna 2003, p. 81; Ziegler A., Ein Werk des Friedens, Munich 1979, p. 133.

[55] Weh L., Stalag VII A - Alpdruck und Schicksal der Stadt Moosburg, in: Keller M. (ed.), Was ist geschehn?, Moosburg 1995, pp. 130-152, p. 138.

[56] POW Camp VII, Gruppe III, „Brief- und Paketpost", Federal Military Archives, RH 49/49, p. 33b.

[57] Report of the SD No. 325 of 12.10.1942, in: Boberach H. (ed.), Meldungen aus dem Reich, Herrsching 1984, pp. 4317f.

[58] Spoerer M., Zwangsarbeit unter dem Hakenkreuz, Munich 2001, pp. 106, 122ff; Speckner H., In der Gewalt des Feindes, Vienna 2003, pp. 47ff; Mommsen H., In deutscher Hand - Der Arbeitseinsatz sowjetischer Kriegsgefangener 1941-1943 in: Haus der Geschichte der Bundesrepublik Deutschland (ed.), Kriegsgefangene, Düsseldorf 1995, pp. 141-147, p. 145.

[59] Transcript of a lecture given by Colonel Nepf to citizens of Moosburg in the Stalag canteen in January 1941, Moosburg Municipal Archives, 06/45, p. 7.

[60] Speckner H., In der Gewalt des Feindes, Vienna 2003, p. 81f.

[61] Moosburg Municipal Archives, Stalag VII A Bildchronik vol. II; Speckner H., In der Gewalt des Feindes, Vienna 2003, p. 48 on the comparable situation in Austria.

[62] Letter from the Brewery Association of Southern Germany to the Mayor of the City of Moosburg, 12.10.1943, Moosburg Municipal Archives, 06/72.

[63] Moosburg Municipal Archives, Stalag VII A Bildchronik vol II.

[64] For example, the City of Moosburg requested large numbers of ration coupons from the Freising Nutrition Office for foodstuffs for the prisoners it employed, Moosburg Municipal Archives, 06/52; 06/58.

[65] Mommsen H., In deutscher Hand, in: Haus der Geschichte der Bundesrepublik Deutschland (ed.), Kriegsgefangene, Düsseldorf 1995, pp. 141-148, p. 146f., using the example of Soviet prisoners. Ziegler, citing Colonel Burger, mentions a case from the area of responsibility of Stalag VII A, Ziegler A., Ein Werk des Friedens, Munich 1979, p. 124.

[66] Leaflet "Verhalten gegenüber Kriegsgefangenen", published by the OKW and the Reich Propaganda Ministry in May 1943, reprinted in Pfahlmann H., Fremdarbeiter und Kriegsgefangene in der deutschen Kriegswirtschaft 1939-1945, Darmstadt 1945, p. 189; leaflet „Verhalten gegenüber Kriegsgefangenen im Arbeitseinsatz" („Behavior towards Prisoners of War in Labor Deployment"), , published by the OKW, the Party Chancellery and the Propaganda Ministry, Federal Military Archives, RH 49/49, p. 8.

[67] Stalag VII A, Gruppe Verwaltung, "A. Verpflegung", Federal Military Archives, RH 49/49, p. 39.

[68] cf. corresponding correspondence between the City of Moosburg and the relevant authorities, for example letter from the town administration to the Freising Nutrition Office dated 25 August 1943, in which ration coupons for foodstuffs were requested for the Gasthaus zur Lände in order to supply 25 Soviet prisoners on work duty for the town, Moosburg Municipal Archives, 06/52.

[69] Mommsen H., In deutscher Hand, in: Haus der Geschichte der Bundesrepublik Deutschland (ed.), Kriegsgefangene, Düsseldorf 1995, p. 141-148, p. 145; Keller R., Das deutsch-russische Forschungsprojekt "Sowjetische Kriegsgefangene" in: Bischof G./Karner S./Stelzl-Marx B. (eds.), Kriegsgefangene des Zweiten Weltkriegs, Vienna 2005, p. 460-475, p. 470ff.

[70] Spoerer M., Zwangsarbeit unter dem Hakenkreuz, Munich 2001, p. 103f.

[71] Spoerer M., Zwangsarbeit unter dem Hakenkreuz, Munich 2001, p. 124f.

[72] Mommsen H., In deutscher Hand, in: Haus der Geschichte der Bundesrepublik Deutschland (ed.), Kriegsgefangene, Düsseldorf 1995, p. 141-147, 146f.

[73] Speckner H., In der Gewalt des Feindes, Vienna 2003, p. 54ff.

[74] Spoerer M., Zwangsarbeit unter dem Hakenkreuz, Munich 2001, p. 136ff; Speckner H., In der Gewalt des Feindes, Vienna 2003, p. 56.

[75] Transcript of a lecture by Colonel Nepf, given to citizens of Moosburg in the Stalag canteen in January 1941, Moosburg Municipal Archives, 06/45, p. 8; POW Camp VII A, Gruppe Verwaltung, Dienstanweisung "Bekleidung", Federal Military Archives, RH 49/49, p. 37b.

[76] Federal Military Archives, RH 49/49, p. 76f.

[77] Explanatory note to reference A, Federal Military Archives, RH 49/49, p. 38.

[78] "Bekleidungsnachweis" with instructions for completion on reverse, Federal Military Archives, RH 49/49, p. 70,70b.

[79] Sample report of loss, Federal Military Archives, RH 49/49, B. 68.

[80] Speckner H., In der Gewalt des Feindes, Vienna 2003, p. 58 with reference to a circular of the Reich Minister of Economics of 16.02.1942 and Sammelmitteilungen und Befehlssammlung OKW No. 11, Federal Military Archives, RW 6/v. 270.

81 Pfahlmann H., Fremdarbeiter und Kriegsgefangene in der deutschen Kriegswirtschaft 1939-1945, Darmstadt 1968, p. 31, 82f.; with regard to Soviet prisoners Mommsen H., In deutscher Hand, in: Haus der Geschichte der Bundesrepublik Deutschland (ed.), Kriegsgefangene, Düsseldorf 1995, p. 141-147, p. 141; Mojonny G., The labor of prisoners of war in Modern Times, Locarro 1955, p. 32.

82 "Der deutsche Soldat in der Kriegsgefangenenbewachung", letter from the OKW, 16.01.1943, Federal Military Archives, RH 49/49, p. 4.

83 Mojonny G., The labor of prisoners of war in Modern Times, Locarro 1955, p. 32; Pfahlmann H., Fremdarbeiter und Kriegsgefangene in der deutschen Kriegswirtschaft 1939-1945, Darmstadt 1968, p. 104.

84 Otto R., Wehrmacht, Gestapo und sowjetische Gefangene im deutschen Reichsgebiet 1941/42, Munich 1998, p. 31 FN 25 with reference to a letter from the command of military district VII dated 22.09 1939.

85 Pfahlmann H., Fremdarbeiter und Kriegsgefangene in der deutschen Kriegswirtschaft 1939-1945, Darmstadt 1968, p. 104ff.

86 Mojonny G., The labor of prisoners of war in Modern Times, Locarno 1955, p. 32; Pfahlmann H., Fremdarbeiter und Kriegsgefangene in der deutschen Kriegswirtschaft 1939-1945, Darmstadt 1968, p. 114f. with details on the procedure; for example, request for 20 unskilled workers by the Moosburg municipal construction office on 14.11.1939, contract between the City of Moosburg and the German Reich, represented by the commandant of the Stalag on the transfer of 20 unskilled workers for road construction of 15.11.1939, Moosburg Municipal Archives, 06/57

87 Spoerer M., Zwangsarbeit unter dem Hakenkreuz, Munich 2001, p. 102; as an example of the sentences in 1940, letter from the administration group of Stalag VII A (Az. Z. 2 f z 2) dated July 8, 1940, Moosburg Municipal Archives, 06/57.

88 Matiello G., Prisoners of War in Germany 1939-1945, Lodi 2001, p. 78.

89 Spoerer M., Zwangsarbeit unter dem Hakenkreuz, Munich 2001, p. 102.

90 POW Camp VII A, Gruppe III, Instruction on the Accommodation of Prisoners on Labor Deployment, Federal Military Archives, RH 49/49, p. 31.

91 Spoerer M., Zwangsarbeit unter dem Hakenkreuz, Munich 2001, p. 164f.; according to Colonel Nepf, an average of 900,000-1,000,000 RM was paid out in 1940, and as much as 1,430,000 RM in December 1940; purchases could be made in nine Moosburg shops with the camp money, transcript of a lecture by Colonel Nepf, to Moosburg citizens in the Stalag canteen in January 1941, Moosburg Municipal Archives, 06/45, p. 8f.

92 Ziegler A., Ein Werk des Friedens, Munich 1979, p. 163.

93 Spoerer M., Zwangsarbeit unter dem Hakenkreuz, Munich 2001, p. 165f.; Working conditions and wages changed again and again, cf. Moosburg Municipal Archives files "Kriegsgefangene in der Landwirtschaft", 06/59.

94 Spoerer M., Zwangsarbeit unter dem Hakenkreuz, Munich 2001, p. 169.

95 Spoerer M., Zwangsarbeit unter dem Hakenkreuz, Munich 2001, p. 175.

96 Mojonny G., The labor of prisoners of war in Modern Times, Locarno 1955, p. 36; Pfahlmann H., Fremdarbeiter und Kriegsgefangene in der deutschen Kriegswirtschaft 1939-1945, Darmstadt 1968, p. 179.

97 Spoerer M., Zwangsarbeit unter dem Hakenkreuz, Munich 2001, p. 168ff.

98 POW Camp VII A, leaflet "Allgemeine Anweisungen für Arbeitseinsatz und Bewachung von Gefangenen", Federal Military Archives, RH 49/49, p. 48; form for the appointment of an auxiliary guard, Federal Military Archives, RH 49-49, p. 51; Spoerer M., Zwangsarbeit unter dem Hakenkreuz, Munich 2001, p. 121.

99 Letter of the OKW dated 26.06.1942, file no. 2 f 24. 17a Chief POW Allg (I)/Org (IIIB) No. 2916/42, Federal Military Archives, RH 49/49, p. 7; leaflet "Der deutsche Soldat in der Kriegsgefangenen–bewachung" dated 16.01.1943, Federal Military Archives, RH 49/49, p. 4f.

100 Memorandum by Mayor Müller dated 21.09.1939, Moosburg Municipal Archives, 06/47.

101 Contract in the file 06/57 of the Municipal Archives Moosburg.

102 File holdings Moosburg Municipal Archives 06/30, 06/31 and 06/58. In weekly lists, the construction company stated the number of prisoners deployed on each day, Moosburg Municipal Archives, Einsatz von Kriegsgefangenen beim Bau des städtischen Hauptkanals, 06/31.

[103] Cf. a corresponding note by the municipal building authority of 28 April 1941, Moosburg Municipal Archives, 06/57.

[104] The deployment and number of prisoners can be seen in letters from the Moosburg town administration to the Freising Food Office dated 20.09.1943 and from autumn 1943 to spring 1944, Moosburg Municipal Archives, 06/52.

[105] This can be seen from a request for blankets by the Moosburg city administration, which cannot be dated exactly, Moosburg city archive, 06/46.

[106] Letter by the company commander of the 6th Company of the Landesschützenbataillon 512 to the mayor of the City of Moosburg dated 07.11.1942, Moosburg Municipal Archives 06/49.

[107] Pfahlmann H., Fremdarbeiter und Kriegsgefangene in der deutschen Kriegswirtschaft 1939-1945, Darmstadt 1968, p. 187.

[108] Leaflet " Der deutsche Soldat in der Kriegsgefangenenbewachung" Federal Military Archives, RH 49/49, p. 5.

[109] Files of the Party Chancellery, quoted from Pfahlmann H., Fremdarbeiter und Kriegsgefangene in der deutschen Kriegswirtschaft 1939-1945, Darmstadt 1968, p. 187.

[110] Files of the Party Chancellery, quoted from Pfahlmann H., Fremdarbeiter und Kriegsgefangene in der deutschen Kriegswirtschaft 1939-1945, Darmstadt 1968, p. 187.

[111] Moosburg Municipal Archives, 06/69.

[112] Pfahlmann H., Fremdarbeiter und Kriegsgefangene in der deutschen Kriegswirtschaft 1939-1945, Darmstadt 1968, p. 187ff.

[113] Leaflet "Verhalten gegenüber Kriegsgefangenen", reprinted in Pfahlmann H., Fremdarbeiter und Kriegsgefangene in der deutschen Kriegswirtschaft 1939-1945, Darmstadt 1968, p. 188.

[114] Letter no. 5663 from the Moosburg police post dated 02.11.1940 to the mayor of the City of Moosburg, Moosburg Municipal Archives, 06/69.

[115] Speckner H., In der Gewalt des Feindes, Vienna 2003, p. 157.

[116] Letter No. 35 from the Moosburg police post dated 07.01.1940 to the Freising District Administrator, Moosburg Municipal Archives, 06/69.

[117] Memorandum dated 04.04.1942, Moosburg Municipal Archives, 06/66.

[118] Leaflet „Verhalten gegenüber Kriegsgefangenen" from 1940, reprinted in Pfahlmann H., Fremdarbeiter und Kriegsgefangene in der deutschen Kriegswirtschaft 1939-1945, Darmstadt 1968, p. 188.

[119] Leaflet "Verhalten gegenüber Kriegsgefangenen im Arbeits– einsatz" ("Behavior towards Prisoners of War in Labor Deployment"), prepared by the OKW, the Party Chancellery, and the Propaganda Ministry, July 1943, Federal Military Archives, RH 49/49, p. 8.

[120] Letter of the Deputy General Command VII A.K. Az I a Kr. Gef.-Nr. 730/40 dated 15.01.1940, Federal Military Archives, RH 49/49, p. 18.

[121] Landesschützenbataillon 512, circular no. 2/43 of 22.02.1943, Moosburg Municipal Archives, 06/48.

[122] POW Camp VII A Camp Regulations of 08.01.1944, Federal Military Archives, RH 49/49, p. 88.

[123] Weh L., Stalag VII A - Alpdruck und Schicksal der Stadt Moosburg in: Keller M. (ed.), Was ist geschehn?, Moosburg 1995, p. 130-152, p. 137.

[124] Speckner H., In der Gewalt des Feindes, Vienna 2003, p. 156.

[125] Landesschützenbataillon 512, circular no. 2/43 of 22.02.1943, Moosburg Municipal Archives, 06/48.

[126] Letter from the mayor of the City of Moosburg dated 22 August 1942 with list of signatures, Moosburg Municipal Archives, 06/69.

[127] Bekanntmachung über das Betreten des Kriegsgefangenenlagers Moosburg vom 23.10.1939, Moosburg Municipal Archives, 06/46.

[128] Ziegler A., Ein Werk des Friedens, Munich 1979.

[129] Ziegler A., Ein Werk des Friedens, Munich 1979, p. 130f., p. 174.

[130] Ziegler A., Ein Werk des Friedens, Munich 1979, p. 46f.; Thus town parish priest Schiml informed the district administrator of Freising on 1944/10/30 that on 12.11.1944 a service for the Catholic Ukrainians would be held in the St. John's Church in Moosburg, Moosburg Municipal Archives, 06/65.

[131] Ziegler A., Ein Werk des Friedens, Munich 1979, p. 48.

[132] Ziegler A., Ein Werk des Friedens, Munich 1979, p. 48ff.

[133] Ziegler A., Ein Werk des Friedens, Munich 1979, p. 93, 101, 103, 157.

[134] Ziegler A., Ein Werk des Friedens, Munich 1979, p. 146f.

[135] Ziegler A., Ein Werk des Friedens, Munich 1979, p. 104ff.

[136] Ziegler A., Ein Werk des Friedens, Munich 1979, p. 108f.

[137] Ziegler A., Ein Werk des Friedens, Munich 1979, p. 38ff.

[138] Ziegler A., Ein Werk des Friedens, Munich 1979, p. 52ff, 143.

[139] Ziegler A., Ein Werk des Friedens, Munich 1979, p. 47, 161f., 185, 210, 248, 252; Moosburg Municipal Archives, Stalag VII A Bildchronik Vol. II

[140] Alckens A., Moosburg Municipal Archives, Bestand Stalag VII A Kulturelles Leben im Stalag; August Alckens was employed as an interpreter in the camp.

[141] Some copies have been preserved in the Moosburg Municipal Archives, fonds Stalag VII A.

[142] Speckner H., In der Gewalt des Feindes, Vienna 2003, p. 91ff.

[143] Moosburg Municipal Archives, Stalag VII A Bildchronik vol II.

[144] Speckner H., In der Gewalt des Feindes, Vienna 2003, p. 63.

[145] Transcript of a lecture given by Colonel Nepf to citizens of Moosburg in the Stalag canteen in January 1941, Moosburg Municipal Archives, 06/45, p. 6ff.

[146] Ziegler A., Ein Werk des Friedens, Munich 1979, p. 44f.; Speckner H., In der Gewalt des Feindes, Vienna 2003, p. 59, 69.

[147] Speckner H., In der Gewalt des Feindes, Vienna 2003, p. 63f., using the example of Stalag XVII B, but in view of the insofar similar situation in the camps, this was probably a general phenomenon. Undated leaflet by the troop and camp doctor of the POW Camp VII A, Federal Military Archives, RH 49/49, p. 42; Ziegler A., Ein Werk des Friedens, Munich 1979, p. 100.

[148] Undated leaflet by the troop and camp doctor of the POW Camp VII A Federal Military Archives, RH 49/49, p. 40.

[149] Undated leaflet by the troop and camp doctor of the POW Camp VII A, Federal Military Archives, RH 49/49, p. 42; Speckner H., In der Gewalt des Feindes, Vienna 2003, p. 70.

[150] Speckner H., In der Gewalt des Feindes, Vienna 2003, p. 70.

[151] Letters from two employees of the card index of Stalag VII A to the City of Moosburg dated 28 May 1947 and 24 May 1947, Moosburg Municipal Archives, 06/36; death certificate for the American prisoner Fred Bradshaw, who died in the camp hospital, received by the City of Moosburg on 23 April 1945, Moosburg Municipal Archives, 06/37.

[152] Letter from an employee of the card index of Stalag VII A to the City of Moosburg, 17.06.1947, Moosburg Municipal Archives, 06/37.

[153] The various lists can be found in the file "Kriegsgefangenenfriedhof Thonstetten" of the Moosburg Municipal Archives, 06/36.

[154] Municipal Archives Moosburg, 06/36.

[155] Ziegler is quoting here a lecture given by Colonel Burger in 1962, Ziegler A., Ein Werk des Friedens, Munich 1979, p. 99; Reither D., Zwischen Vernichtung und Widerstand – Das Leben sowjetischer Gefangener im Stalag VII A Moosburg, in: Reither D./Rausch K./Abstiens E./Fößmeier C. (edd), Auf den Spuren verlorener Identitäten, Moosburg 2018, S. 9-172, S. 87.

[156] List of deceased British prisoners, Moosburg Municipal Archives, 06/68.

[157] List of deceased US prisoners, Moosburg Municipal Archives, 06/37.

[158] Cf. also the lists of Soviet prisoners buried in the Moosburg cemetery and the Oberreit cemetery, Moosburg Municipal Archives, 06/42.

[159] List of deceased French prisoners, Moosburg Municipal Archives, 06/39.

[160] List of deceased Italian prisoners, Moosburg Municipal Archives, 06/40.

[161] List of deceased Yugoslav prisoners, Moosburg Municipal Archives, 06/41.

[162] List of deceased British prisoners, Moosburg Municipal Archives, 06/68.

[163] List of deceased US prisoners, Moosburg Municipal Archives, 06/37.

[164] Ziegler A., Ein Werk des Friedens, Munich 1979, p. 100.

[165] Mommsen H., In deutscher Hand, in: Haus der Geschichte der Bundesrepublik Deutschland (ed.), Kriegsgefangene, Düsseldorf 1995, p. 141-147, p. 141.

[166] Otto R., Wehrmacht, Gestapo und sowjetische Gefangene im deutschen Reichsgebiet 1941/42, Munich 1998, p. 271 on the conditions in the "Russian camps" on German Reich territory. On Bergen-Belsen Keller R., Das deutsch-russische Forschungsprojekt "Sowjetische Kriegsgefangene" in: Bischof G./Karner S./Stelzl-

Marx B. (eds.), Kriegsgefangene des Zweiten Weltkriegs, Vienna 2005, p. 460-475, p. 472.

167 List of deceased British prisoners, Moosburg Municipal Archives, 06/68.

168 Federal Military Archives, RH 49/49, p. 1.

169 Speckner H., In der Gewalt des Feindes, Vienna 2003, p. 58.

170 Speckner H., In der Gewalt des Feindes, Vienna 2003, p. 59; letter from an employee of the card index of Stalag VII A to the City of Moosburg dated 24.05.1947, Moosburg Municipal Archives, 06/36; Ziegler A., Ein Werk des Friedens, Munich 1979, p. 79ff, 93.

171 Letter from an employee of the card index of Stalag VII A to the City of Moosburg dated 24.05.1947, Moosburg Municipal Archives, 06/36; list of Soviet prisoners buried in the Oberreit cemetery from 1984, Moosburg Municipal Archives, 06/36.

172 List of deceased British prisoners, Moosburg Municipal Archives, 06/68.

173 In detail on this and on the ideological background Streit C., Keine Kameraden, Bonn 2001, p. 72ff.

174 Otto R., Wehrmacht, Gestapo und sowjetische Kriegsgefangene im deutschen Reichsgebiet 1941/42, Munich 1998, p. 48ff, 268; Streim A., Sowjetische Gefangene in Hitlers Vernichtungskrieg, Heidelberg 1982, p. 30ff.

175 Otto R., Wehrmacht, Gestapo und sowjetische Kriegsgefangene im deutschen Reichsgebiet 1941/42, Munich 1998, p. 208f. There were also controversies between the Wehrmacht and the Gestapo in Wehrkreis II Stettin, but almost nothing is known about them.

176 In great detail Otto R., Wehrmacht, Gestapo und sowjetische Kriegsgefangene im deutschen Reichsgebiet 1941/42, Munich 1998, p. 208ff.; Streit C., Keine Kameraden, Bonn 2001, p. 95ff; Streim A., Sowjetische Gefangene in Hitlers Vernichtungskrieg, Heidelberg 1982, p. 36ff.

177 The records are printed almost in their entirety in: Secretariat of the International Military Tribunal (ed.), Der Prozess gegen die Hauptkriegsverbrecher vor dem Internationalen Militärgerichtshof, Vol. XXXVIII, Nuremberg 1949, p. 419-498 (Exhibit 178-R).

178 Proceedings of the Public Prosecutor's Office Munich I, Az 1 Js Gen. 119-125/50, State Archives Munich Staatsanwaltschaft No. 20988.

179 Keller R., Sowjetische Kriegsgefangene im Deutschen Reich 1941/42, Göttingen 2011, p. 90.

180 Testimony of Colonel Nepf in the proceedings of the Public Prosecutor's Office Munich I, File No. 1 Js Gen. 119-125/50, State Archives Munich Staatsanwaltschaft No. 20988, p. 264. Some of the prisoners were already on work duty, file note of the Gestapo office Munich dated 12.09.1941, Secretariat of the International Military Tribunal (ed.), Der Prozess gegen die Hauptkriegsverbrecher, Nuremberg 1949, Vol. XXXVIII, p. 419f.

181 Report of the Munich Gestapo Office of 16.01.1941, in: Secretariat of the International Military Tribunal (ed,), Der Prozess gegen die Hauptkriegsverbrecher, Nuremberg 1949, Vol. XXXVIII, p. 440f.

182 Telex No. 18193 of the Dresden Gestapo Office of 25 September 1941 and No. 18149 of 24 September 1941 of the Halle Gestapo Office to the Munich Gestapo Office, in: Secretariat of the International Military Tribunal (ed.), Der Prozess gegen der Hauptkriegsverbrecher, Nuremberg 1949, Vol. XXXVIII, p. 422f.

183 Report of the Munich Gestapo Office of 16.01.1942, in: Secretariat of the International Military Tribunal (ed.), Der Prozess gegen die Hauptkriegsverbrecher, Nuremberg 1949, Vol. XXXVIII, p. 441; Otto R., Wehrmacht, Gestapo und sowjetische Kriegsgefangene im deutschen Reichsgebiet 1941/42, Munich 1998, p. 211 FN 254.

184 Testimony of a Wehrmacht interpreter used during the interrogations in the proceedings of the Public Prosecutor's Office Munich I, File No. 1 Js Gen. 119-125/50, State Archives Munich Staatsanwaltschaft No. 20988, p. 265.

185 On the beginning of the task force's activities, report of the Munich Gestapo office of 26 November 1941, "Der Prozess gegen die Hauptkriegsverbrecher", Nuremberg 1949, Vol. XXXVIII, p. 447; on the number of personnel, statement of a Gestapo official involved in the segregations in the proceedings of the Public Prosecutor's Office Munich I, File No. 1 Js Gen. 119-125/50, State Archives Munich Staatsanwaltschaft No. 20988, p. 290 RS.

186 Statement by Hauptmann Hörmann in the proceedings of the Public Prosecutor's Office Munich I, file no. 1 Js Gen. 119-125/50, State Archives Munich, Staatsanwaltschaft No. 20988, p. 252; testimony of a Wehrmacht interpreter used during the interrogations in the proceedings Public Prosecutor's Office Munich I, Az 1 Js Gen. 119-125/50, State Archives Munich Staatsanwaltschaft No. 20988, p. 303.

187 Report of the Munich Gestapo office of 15 November 1941, Der Prozess gegen die Hauptkriegsverbrecher, Nuremberg 1949, Vol.

XXXVIII, p. 424f.; on the course of the checks, statement by a Wehrmacht interpreter in the proceedings of the Public Prosecutor's Office Munich I, File No. 1 Js Gen. 119-125/50, State Archives Munich Staatsanwaltschaft No. 20988, p. 269ff; testimony of two Gestapo officials involved in the proceedings of the Public Prosecutors Office Munich I, Az 1 Js Gen. 119-125/50, State Archives Munich Staatsanwaltschaft No. 20988, p. 259ff, 290f; testimony of Major Meinel in the proceedings of the Public Prosecutor's Office Munich I, file no. 1 Js Gen. 119-125/50, State Archives Munich Staatsanwaltschaft. No. 20988, p. 316.

[188] Report of the Munich Gestapo Office of 15.11.1941, Secretariat of the International Military Tribunal (ed.), Der Prozess gegen die Hauptkriegsverbrecher, Nuremberg 1949, Vol. XXXVIII, p. 424ff.

[189] This can be inferred above all from Nepf's and Hörmann's statements in the proceedings of the Public Prosecutor's Office Munich I, Az 1 Js Gen. 119-125/50, State Archives Munich Staatsanwaltschaft No. 20988, p. 252, 264 and from their further proceedings.

[190] Nepf's and Hörmann's statements in the proceedings of the Public Prosecutor's Office Munich I, Az 1 Js Gen. 119-125/50, State Archives Munich Staatsanwaltschaft No. 20988, p. 252, 264.

[191] Statement of the interpreter in the proceedings of the Public Prosecutor's Office Munich I, Az 1 Js Gen. 119-125/50, State Archives Munich Staatsanwaltschaft No. 20988, p. 265ff.

[192] Otto R., Wehrmacht, Gestapo und sowjetische Kriegsgefangene im deutschen Reichsgebiet 1941/42, Munich 1998, p. 224.

[193] Hörmann's testimony in the Public Prosecutor's Office Munich I proceedings, Az. 1 Js Gen. 119-125/50, State Archives Munich Staatsanwaltschaft No. 20988, p. 252; the Gestapo then no longer negociated with him, but only with Colonel Nepf; testimony of one of the Wehrmacht interpreters used in the proceedings of the Public Prosecutors Office Munich I, Az. 1 Js Gen. 119-125/50, State Archives Munich Staatsanwaltschaft No. 20988, p. 266RS; testimony of Major General v. Saur in proceedings of the Public Prosecutors Office Munich I, Az. 1 Js Gen. 119-125/50, State Archives Munich Staatsanwaltschaft No. 20988, p. 299; Report of the Munich Gestapo Office of 17 Dec. 1941, Secretariat of the International Military Tribunal (ed.), Der Prozess gegen die Hauptkriegsverbrecher, Nuremberg 1949, Vol. XXXVIII, p. 490ff;

[194] Meinel's testimony in the Public Prosecutor's Office Munich I proceedings, Az. 1 Js Gen. 119-125/50, State Archives Munich Staatsanwaltschaft No. 20988, p. 316.

[195] Meinel's testimony in the proceedings of the Public Prosecutor's Office Munich I, Az. 1 Js Gen. 119-125/50, State Archives Munich, Staatsanwaltschaft No. 20988, p. 316; Otto R., Wehrmacht, Gestapo und sowjetische Kriegsgefangene im deutschen Reichsgebiet 1941/42, Munich 1998, p. 213 with evaluation of further investigation files.

[196] Telex of the Reich Security Main Office No. 21231 of 13.11.1941 to the Gestapo Office Munich, in: Secretariat of the International Military Tribunal (ed.), Der Prozess gegen die Hauptkriegsverbrecher, Nuremberg 1949, Vol. XXXVIII, p. 423f.

[197] Reports of the Munich Gestapo Office of 15.11.1941 and 17.12.1941, in: Secretariat of the International Military Tribunal (ed.), Der Prozess gegen die Hauptkriegsverbrecher, Nuremberg 1949, Vol. XXXVIII, p. 424ff., 490ff.

[198] Report of the Munich Gestapo Office of 24.11.1941 and Major Meinel's statement on the discussion, in: Secretariat of the International Military Tribunal (ed.), Der Prozess gegen die Hauptkriegsverbrecher, Nuremberg 1949, Vol. XXXVIII, p. 432ff., 439f.

[199] Report of the Munich Gestapo Office of 26 November 1941, in: Secretariat of the International Military Tribunal (ed.), Der Prozess gegen die Hauptkriegsverbrecher, Nuremberg 1949, Vol. XXXVIII, p. 447ff; on the number of POW brought to Dachau, Otto R., Wehrmacht, Gestapo und sowjetische Kriegsgefangene im deutschen Reichsgebiet 1941/42, Munich 1998, p. 217.

[200] Statements by Hörmann and Nepf in the Public Prosecutor's Office Munich I proceedings, Az 1 Js Gen. 119-125/50, State Archives Munich Staatsanwaltschaft No. 20988, p. 252f., 264f.

[201] This can be concluded from a letter from v. Saur to the Gestapo office in Munich dated 14.01.1942, file no. BXI/12 No. 15 geh. (in: Secretariat of the International Military Tribunal (ed.), Der Prozess gegen die Hauptkriegsverbrecher, Nuremberg 1949, vol. XXXVIII, p. 443f.). In this letter v. Saur refers to a letter of the Gestapo of 09.01.1941 to the commandant of Stalag VII A, he refuses to hand over the remaining prisoners; so also Otto R., Wehrmacht, Gestapo und sowjetische Kriegsgefangene im deutschen Reichsgebiet 1941/42, Munich 1998, p. 217.

[202] Report of the Gestapo Office Munich of 16.01.1942 and Report of the Gestapo Office Regensburg to the Reich Security Main Office of 19.01.1942, in: Secretariat of the International Military Tribunal (ed.), Der Prozess gegen die Hauptkriegsverbrecher, Nuremberg 1949, Vol. XXXVIII p. 440ff, 452ff.

203 Otto R., Wehrmacht, Gestapo und sowjetische Kriegsgefangene im deutschen Reichsgebiet 1941/42, Munich 1998, p. 224.

204 Otto R., Wehrmacht, Gestapo und sowjetische Kriegsgefangene im deutschen Reichsgebiet 1941/42, Munich 1998, p. 218f.

205 Letter from the Munich Gestapo Office to the Reich Security Main Office, 28.01.1942, in: Secretariat of the International Military Tribunal (ed.), Der Prozess gegen die Hauptkriegsverbrecher, Nuremberg 1949, Vol. XXXVIII, p. 474f.

206 Letter from the Munich Gestapo Office to the Reich Security Main Office dated 26.01.1942, in: Secretariat of the International Military Tribunal (ed.), Der Prozess gegen die Hauptkriegsverbrecher, Nuremberg 1949, Vol. XXXVIII, p. 467ff.

207 Otto R., Wehrmacht, Gestapo und sowjetische Kriegsgefangene im deutschen Reichsgebiet 1941/42, Munich 1998, p. 220f., 268.

208 On this and generally on the procedure, v. Saur's letter of 26 February 1942 (file no. B X I / 12 No. 57 geh) to the Mannschaftsstammlager VII A Moosburg, in: Secretariat of the International Military Tribunal (ed.), Der Prozess gegen die Hauptkriegsverbrecher, Nuremberg 1949, Vol. XXXVIII, p. 486f.

209 Nepf's and Hörmann's statements in the proceedings of the Public Prosecutor's Office Munich I, Az. 1 Js Gen. 119-125/50, State Archives Munich Staatsanwaltschaft No. 20988, p. 264, 301 RS; Nepf states that he was commandant of the Stalag until 5 January 1943.

210 Otto R., Wehrmacht, Gestapo und sowjetische Kriegsgefangene im deutschen Reichsgebiet 1941/42, Munich 1998, p. 221.

211 Meinel's testimony in the Public Prosecutor's Office Munich I proceedings, file Az. Js Gen. 119-125/50, State Archives Munich Staatsanwaltschaft No. 20988, p. 316 RS.

212 Otto R., Wehrmacht, Gestapo und sowjetische Kriegsgefangene im deutschen Reichsgebiet 1941/42, Munich 1998, p. 228f.

213 Nepf was 65 years old in 1941, Meinel 64 years old, v. Saur also 65 years old, only Hörmann, at 46, belonged to a younger generation, cf. the corresponding statements in the Public Prosecutor's Office Munich I proceedings, Az 1 Js Gen. 119-125/50, State Archives Munich Staatsanwaltschaft No. 20988, p. 264, 316, 299, 252.

214 Testimony in the Public Prosecutor's Office Munich I proceedings, Az. 1 Js Gen. 119-125/50, State Archives Munich Staatsanwaltschaft No. 20988, p. 268.

215 Hörmann's testimony in the Public Prosecutor's Office Munich I proceedings, Az. 1 Js Gen. 119-125/50, State Archives Munich Staatsanwaltschaft No. 20988, p. 253, 301RS.

216 Exemplary here is the statement of the Commanding General of the Deputy General Command VII, General der Artillerie v. Wachenfeld, v. Saur's highest-ranking superior on the spot. V. Wachenfeld states that v. Saur had told him about the segregations and that he assumed that the prisoners would be shot; he had also protested to General Reinecke. V. Wachenfeld then states that he had discussed the situation with v. Saur, and that both had concluded that there was now no further course. The idea of refusing the order is not addressed by v. Wachenfeld, statement of v. Wachenfeld in the proceedings Munich Public Prosecutor's Office I, Az 1 Js Gen. 119-125/50, State Archives Munich Staatsanwaltschaft No. 20988, p. 304; also in the statements of the officers involved the refusal of orders is not mentioned.

217 Pfahlmann H., Fremdarbeiter und Kriegsgefangene in der deutschen Kriegswirtschaft 1939-1945, Darmstadt 1968, p. 183f.

218 Cf. the numerous corresponding letters to the municipal administration of Moosburg, for example Moosburg Municipal Archives, 06/67.

219 Speckner H., In der Gewalt des Feindes, Vienna 2003, p. 111ff.

220 In Moosburg, too, numerous persons were appointed auxiliary guardsmen to guard prisoners of war, for example employees of those factories where prisoners were on work duty, exemplary list of 06.06.1941 with 70 names, Moosburg Municipal Archives, 06/55.

221 Copy of the order of the Reichsführer SS and Chief of the German Police in the Reich Ministry of the Interior, Az O-Kdo I O (4) Nr. 6/42 of 17.01.1942 to the Commander of the Gendarmerie at the District President in Munich, from there with comments as letter Nr. 520 (as a copy) to the Freising Gendarmerie District Commander, from there as letter Nr. 162 to the Mayor of the City of Moosburg, Moosburg Municipal Archives, 06/67.

222 Speckner H., In der Gewalt des Feindes, Vienna 2003, p. 74f.

223 Note by the municipal treasurer's office dated July 8, 1942, Moosburg Municipal Archives, 06/57; the municipal treasurer's office suggested returning the two prisoners to the camp in order to "avoid trouble".

[224] Instruction "Kontrollmaßnahmen zur Verhinderung von Fluchten am Wochenende" (Control Measures to Prevent Escapes at Weekends), Federal Military Archives, RH 49/49, p. 27. Colonel Burger's order is not dated, but Colonel Burger refers to the order A.H.M. 1943 Anschr. 867 Ziffer 105 with regard to the leave regulations of the guards, so that Colonel Burger's order must have been issued in 1943 or later. There were also leaflets on how to write an escape report, Federal Military Archives, RH 49/49, p. 25, 26f.

[225] Pfahmann H., Fremdarbeiter und Kriegsgefangene in der deutschen Kriegswirtschaft 1939-1945, Darmstadt 1968, p. 183f.; In a leaflet "Allgemeine Anweisung für Arbeitseinsatz und Bewachung von Kriegsgefangenen" of Stalag VII A it says "Bei sowjetischen Kriegsgefangenen immer ohne Anruf schießen" (With Soviet prisoners of war always shoot without a call), Federal Military Archives, RH 49/49, p. 48b.

[226] "Merkblatt für den Kommandoführer bei Todesfällen von Kriegsgefangenen" (Leaflet for the Commanding Officer in Cases of Death of Prisoners of War), Federal Military Archives, RH 49/49, p. 1f

[227] Ziegler A., Ein Werk des Friedens, Munich 1979, p. 99; however, the camp administration of Stalag VII A tried as far as possible to prevent prisoners from entering the sphere of influence of the Gestapo and SS, testimony of the Counterintelligence officer of Stalag VII A, Hauptmann Hörmann, in the proceedings of the Public Prosecutor's Office Munich I, Az 1 Js Gen. 119-125/50, State Archives Munich Staatsanwaltschaft No. 20988, p. 252 RS.

[228] Ziegler A., Ein Werk des Friedens, Munich 1979, p. 95f.; list of deceased British prisoners, Moosburg Municipal Archives, 06/68; list of deceased US prisoners, Moosburg Municipal Archives, 06/67.

[229] Instruction "Kontrollmaßnahmen zur Verhinderung von Fluchten am Wochenende" (Control Measures to Prevent Escapes at Weekends), Federal Military Archives, RH 49/49 p. 27.

[230] Ziegler A., Ein Werk des Friedens, Munich 1979, p. 97, 155.

[231] Leaflet "Verhalten gegenüber Kriegsgefangenen im Arbeitseinsatz" ("Behavior towards Prisoners of War in Labor Deployment"), prepared in cooperation between the OKW, the Party Chancellery, and the Propaganda Ministry, 16 July 1943, Federal Military Archives, RH 49/49, p. 8.

[232] POW Camp VII A, leaflet for disciplinary punishment of prisoners, Federal Military Archives, RH 49/49, p. 9f.; Speckner H., In der Gewalt des Feindes, Vienna 2003, p. 110.

[233] Ziegler A., Ein Werk des Friedens, Munich 1979, p. 137.

[234] POW Camp VII A, leaflet for disciplinary punishment of prisoners, Federal Military Archives, RH 49/49, p. 9f.

[235] Speckner H., In der Gewalt des Feindes, Vienna 2003, p. 136ff.

[236] „Allgemeine Anweisung für Arbeitseinsatz und Bewachung von Kriegsgefangenen" (General Instruction for the Employment and Guarding of Prisoners of War) of Stalag VII A Federal Military Archives, RH 49/49, p. 48b; letter of the OKW dated 26.06.1942, Az. 2 f 24.17a Chief POW Allg (I)/Org (IIIB) No. 2916/42, Federal Military Archives, RH 49/49, p. 7.

[237] List of deceased British prisoners, Moosburg Municipal Archives, 06/68.

[238] Speckner H., In der Gewalt des Feindes, Vienna 2003, p. 136f. based on numerous examples; Ziegler A., Ein Werk des Friedens, Munich 1979, p. 95f.

[239] Streim A., Sowjetische Gefangene in Hitlers Vernichtungskrieg, Heidelberg 1982, p. 103ff.; Speckner H., In der Gewalt des Feindes, Vienna 2003, p. 139ff. especially on the activities of this group in Austria and its cooperation with other resistance groups there.

[240] Letter from the chief confidant of the French prisoners in Stalag VII A, J. Grospiron, to the City of Moosburg from 1982, Moosburg Municipal Archives, Stalag VII A Berichte Beginn-Ende, p. 12ff.

[241] On the military trend in the last years of the war Bullock A., Hitler, Düsseldorf 1961, p. 775ff.; Bullock A., Hitler und Stalin, Munich 1998, p. 1130ff.; Churchill W., Der Zweite Weltkrieg, Bern 1985, p. 986, 1036, 1065; On the situation in Berlin Bullock A., Hitler, Düsseldorf 1961, p. 792ff, Bullock A., Hitler und Stalin Munich 1998, p. 1157; Fest J., Der Untergang, Hamburg 2003.

[242] Ziegler W., Bayern im Übergang. Vom Kriegsende zur Besatzung 1945, in: Pfister P. (ed.), Das Ende des Zweiten Weltkriegs im Erzbistum München und Freising part I, Munich 2005, p. 33-104, p. 49f.; Albrecht D./Gelberg K. (ed.), Das Neue Bayern - Handbuch der Bayerischen Geschichte begründet von Max Spindler, vol. IV part 1, Munich 2003, p. 635ff.

[243] Wehrmachtsberichte vom 27-30.04.1945, dtv (ed.), Munich 1985, vol. 3, p. 558-562.

244 Diem V., Die Freiheitsaktion Bayern, Kallmünz 2013, p. 23ff; Henke K., Die amerikanische Besetzung Deutschlands, Munich 1995, p. 765.

245 Albrecht D./Gelberg K. (eds.), Das Neue Bayern - Handbuch der Bayerischen Geschichte begründet von Max Spindler, vol. IV 1st part volume, Munich 2003, p. 636f.

246 Ziegler A., Ein Werk des Friedens, Munich 1979, p. 85.

247 Weh L., Stalag VII A - Alpdruck und Schicksal der Stadt Moosburg, in: Keller M. (ed.), Was ist geschehn?, Moosburg 1995, p. 130-152, p. 143f.

248 Ziegler A., Ein Werk des Friedens, Munich 1979, p. 84; Weh L., Stalag VII A - Alpdruck und Schicksal der Stadt Moosburg, in: Keller M. (ed.), Was ist geschehn?, Moosburg 1995, p. 130-152, p. 144.

249 Report of the town parish priest Alois Schiml, in: Pfister P. (ed.), Das Ende des Zweiten Weltkriegs im Erzbistum München und Freising, part II, Munich 2005, p. 842-848, p. 843; report of Major Koller's experience from 01.04-01.05.1945, Moosburg Municipal Archives, Stalag VII A Berichte Beginn-Ende p. 2.

250 Report on Major Koller's experiences from 01.04-01.05.1945, Moosburg Municipal Archives, Stalag VII A Berichte Beginn-Ende p. 2.

251 Report on Major Koller's experiences from 01.04-01.05.1945, Moosburg Municipal Archives, Stalag VII A Berichte Beginn-Ende p. 2; Ziegler A., Ein Werk des Friedens, Munich 1979, p. 229.

252 Report on Major Koller's experiences from 01.04-01.05.1945, Moosburg Municipal Archives, Stalag VII A Berichte Beginn-Ende p. 3.

253 Colonel Burger quoting an unidentified Red Cross report, Report of Colonel Burger, Moosburg Municipal Archives Stalag VII A Berichte Beginn-Ende, p. 7.

254 Burger gives the figures 60,000 and 70,000 without further explanation in his report on the end of the war, report of Colonel Burger, Moosburg Municipal Archives Stalag VII A Berichte Beginn-Ende, p. 4, 6.

255 Ziegler A., Ein Werk des Friedens, Munich 1979, p. 229.

256 Colonel Burger quoting vol. 5 No. 39 of the Army Times, 05.05.1945, report of Colonel Burger, Moosburg Municipal Archives Stalag VII A Berichte Beginn-Ende, p. 7.

257 Matiello G., Prisoners of War in Germany 1939-1945, Lodi 2003, p. 78.

258 Weh L., Stalag VII A - Alpdruck und Schicksal der Stadt Moosburg, in: Keller M (ed.), Was ist geschehn?, Moosburg 1995, p. 130-152, p. 143f.; Weh quotes here an unspecified report of Colonel Burger.

259 Moosburg Municipal Archives, Stalag VII A Bildchronik vol II.

260 Matiello G., Prisoners of War in Germany 1939-1945, Lodi 2003, p. 78.

261 Speckner H., In der Gewalt des Feindes, Vienna 2003, p. 36; even barracks that had previously been used for libraries or for storing Red Cross parcels now had to be cleared for housing prisoners.

262 Report of the town parish priest Alois Schiml, in: Pfister P. (ed.), Das Ende des Zweiten Weltkriegs im Erzbistum München und Freising, part II, Munich 2005, p. 842-848, p. 843; Father Schiml also reports that the people of Moosburg had tried to improve the situation of the prisoners with food donations, he speaks of countless hundredweight of food. Colonel Burger does not mention such donations.

263 Weh L., Stalag VII A - Alpdruck und Schicksal der Stadt Moosburg, in: Keller M. (ed.), Was ist geschehn?, Moosburg 1995, p. 130-152, p. 139; Weh quotes an unspecified report by Colonel Burger.

264 Report on Major Kollers' experiences from 01.04-01.05.1945, Moosburg Municipal Archives, Stalag VII A Berichte Beginn-Ende p.1; report by Colonel Burger, Moosburg Municipal Archives, Stalag VII A Berichte Beginn-Ende, p. 1.

265 Report on Major Koller's experience from 01.04-01.05.1945, Moosburg Municipal Archives, Stalag VII A Berichte Beginn-Ende, p. 3; report of Colonel Burger, Moosburg Municipal Archives, Stalag VII A Berichte Beginn-Ende, p. 2. Whether both Burger as camp commander and Koller as combat commander of Moosburg initially each took the decision to surrender without a fight or whether they developed this plan together is not clear from the reports of the two officers. Father Schiml writes that Mayor Müller was also determined not to defend Moosburg, Report of the Town parish priest Alois Schiml, in: Pfister P. (ed.), Das Ende des Zweiten Weltkriegs im Erzbistum München und Freising, Part II, Munich 2005, p. 842-848, p. 843. Koller and Burger often mention each other in reports and describe the intensive cooperation, but Mayor Müller is not mentioned in this context.

266 "Befehl zum Sperreinsatz" of the commander of the Pionier-Ersatz- und Ausbildungs-Bataillon 7, quoted from Brückner J., Kriegsende in Bayern 1945, Freiburg 1987, p. 185.

[267] Report on Major Koller's experiences from 01.04-01.05.1945, Moosburg Municipal Archives, Stalag VII A Berichte Beginn-Ende p. 3.

[268] War Diary of the Southern Command (B) in: Schramm P.E. (ed.), Kriegstagebuch des Oberkommandos der Wehrmacht vol. IV 2nd half volume, Frankfurt 1961, p. 1459. On 22.04.1945, the Wehrmacht Leadership Staff divided into groups A and B. A was responsible for the northern area, B moved from enclosed Berlin to Berchtesgaden by 23/24.04.1945.

[269] Report of Colonel Burger, Moosburg Municipal Archives Stalag VII A Berichte Beginn-Ende p. 2. It is not clear from Burgers' account whether the order was issued by the Wehrmacht Leadership Staff or by the command of military district VII, but due to the chronological sequence it seems likely that the command of military district issued the cited order.

[270] Brückner J., Kriegsende in Bayern 1945, Freiburg 1987, p. 211, 278.

[271] Report of Colonel Burger, Moosburg Municipal Archives Stalag VII A Berichte Beginn-Ende, p. 1.

[272] Report of Colonel Burger, Moosburg Municipal Archives Stalag VII A Berichte Beginn-Ende, p. 2; Brückner J., Kriegsende in Bayern 1945, Freiburg 1987, p. 278.

[273] Report of Colonel Burger, Moosburg Municipal Archives Stalag VII A Berichte Beginn-Ende, p. 2.

[274] Report of Colonel Burger, Moosburg Municipal Archives Stalag VII A Berichte Beginn-Ende, p. 2; For the details of the Freiheitsaktion Bayern and its networking with other resistance groups and their actions, see Diem V., Die Freiheitsaktion Bayern, Kallmünz 2013.

[275] Report on Major Kollers' experiences from 01.04-01.05.1945, Moosburg Municipal Archives, Stalag VII A Berichte Beginn-Ende, p. 3; report by Colonel Burgers, Moosburg Municipal Archives, Stalag VII A Berichte Beginn-Ende, p. 3f.

[276] Keller M., Die Rettung der Amperbrücke, in: dies. (ed.), Was ist geschehn?, Moosburg 1995, p. 68f.

[277] Report of Colonel Burger, Moosburg Municipal Archives Stalag VII A Berichte Beginn-Ende, p. 4f.

[278] Report of Colonel Burger, Moosburg Municipal Archives Stalag VII A Berichte Beginn-Ende, p. 5; Major Koller does state that he was told from Stalag that a neutral zone Mauern, Volkmannsdorf, Thorstetten had been agreed with the Americans in which no fighting was to take place, report on Major Koller's experience from 01.04. - 01.05.1945, Moosburg Municipal Archives, Stalag VII A Berichte Beginn-Ende p. 4. However, in view of the clear statements of Colonel Burger, who was more closely involved in the negotiations, this must have been a misunderstanding on Koller's part.

[279] Report of Colonel Burger, Moosburg Municipal Archives Stalag VII A Berichte Beginn-Ende, p. 5.

[280] Report of Colonel Burger, Moosburg Municipal Archives Stalag VII A Berichte Beginn-Ende, p. 5.

[281] On the tense situation in these days with the XIII SS Corps, which repeatedly led to retreats, Brückner J., Kriegsende in Bayern 1945, Freiburg 1987, p. 185, 211.

[282] Report on Major Koller's experiences from 01.04-01.05.1945, Moosburg Municipal Archives, Stalag VII A Berichte Beginn-Ende p. 4.

[283] Report by Colonel Burger, Moosburg Municipal Archives Stalag VII A Berichte Beginn-Ende, p. 6; Report on Major Koller's experience from 01.04-01.05.1945, Moosburg Municipal Archives, Stalag VII A Berichte Beginn-Ende p. 4; Pastor Schiml reports that in the night of 29.04. American negotiators had been in the town and had agreed with Mayor Müller and Colonel Burger on a surrender without a fight, report of the town parish priest Alois Schiml, in: Pfister P. (ed.), Das Ende des Zweiten Weltkriegs im Erzbistum München und Freising, part II, Munich 2005, p. 842-848, p. 843. This may be wrong. Colonel Burger does not report such negotiations in Moosburg, neither does Major Koller. It seems extremely unlikely, especially against the background of the military situation, that the US troops would have agreed to this. Pastor Schiml, who was obviously not present at the negotiations, seems to confuse the processes here.

[284] Report on Major Koller's experiences from 01.04-01.05.1945, Moosburg Municipal Archives, Stalag VII A Reports Beginn-Ende p. 5; Alckens A., Ein Tagebuch (29 April-22 May 1945), in: Keller M (ed.), Was ist geschehn?, Moosburg 1995, p. 87-129, p. 88.

[285] Report on Major Koller's experience from 01.04-01.05.1945, Moosburg Municipal Archives, Stalag VII A Berichte Beginn-Ende p. 6; report by the town parish priest Alois Schiml, in: Pfister P. (ed.), Das Ende des Zweiten Weltkriegs im Erzbistum München und Freising, part II, Munich 2005, p. 842-848, p. 844f.

[286] Alckens A., Ein Tagebuch (29 April-22 May 1945), in: Keller M. (ed.), Was ist geschehn?, Moosburg 1995, p. 87-129, p. 89.

[287] Report by Colonel Burger, Moosburg Municipal Archives Stalag VII A Berichte Beginn-Ende, p. 6f; Alckens A., Ein Tagebuch (29 April-22 May 1945), in: Keller M. (ed.), Was ist geschehn?, Moosburg 1995, p. 87-129, p. 88f.

[288] Report of Colonel Burger, Moosburg Municipal Archives Stalag VII A Berichte Beginn-Ende, p. 7.

[289] Alckens A., Ein Tagebuch (29 April-22 May 1945), in: Keller M. (ed.), Was ist geschehn?, Moosburg 1995, p. 87-129, p. 89f.

[290] Report on Major Koller's experiences from 01.04-01.05.1945, Moosburg Municipal Archives, Stalag VII A Berichte Beginn-Ende p. 7f.; Alckens A., Ein Tagebuch (29 April-22 May 1945), in: Keller M. (ed.), Was ist geschehn?, Moosburg 1995, p. 87-129, p. 91.

[291] Report of the town parish priest Alois Schiml, in: Pfister P. (ed.), Das Ende des Zweiten Weltkriegs im Erzbistum München und Freising, part II, Munich 2005, p. 842-848, p. 845.

[292] Report of the town parish priest Alois Schiml, in: Pfister P. (ed.), Das Ende des Zweiten Weltkriegs im Erzbistum München und Freising, part II, Munich 2005, p. 842-848, p. 845f.

[293] Report of the town parish priest Alois Schiml, in: Pfister P. (ed.), Das Ende des Zweiten Weltkriegs im Erzbistum München und Freising, part II, Munich 2005, p. 842-848, p. 846ff.; Schiml's accounts were confirmed by the cathedral vicar Frei, who immediately after the end of the war made an inspection trip through the area of the archdiocese Munich-Freising, Stichpunktartiger Bericht des Domvikars Friedrich Frei, in: Pfister P. (ed.), Das Ende des Zweiten Weltkriegs im Erzbistum München und Freising part I, Munich 2005, p. 159.

[294] Report of the town parish priest Alois Schiml, in: Pfister P. (ed.), Das Ende des Zweiten Weltkriegs im Erzbistum München und Freising, part II, Munich 2005, p. 842-848, p. 846ff.

[295] Ziegler A., Ein Werk des Friedens, Munich 1979, p. 232.

[296] Diem V., Die Freiheitsaktion Bayern, Kallmünz 2013, p. 33; Henke K, Die amerikanische Besetzung Deutschlands, Munich 1995, p. 935ff; On the events in the last days of the war, especially the tactical actions of the US forces, cf. Brückner J., Kriegsende in Bayern 1945, Freiburg 1987, p. 246f.

Abbreviations

Gestapo	Geheime Staatspolizei	Secrete State Police
ICRC	International Commitee of the Red Cross	
OKW	Oberkommando der Wehrmacht	Wehrmacht General Command
RSHA	Reichssicherheitshauptamt	Reich's Security Main Office
Stalag	Mannschafts**stamm**lag**er	Base Camp for enlisted men and non-commissioned officers

List of sources and literature

I. Sources:

1. Unprinted sources

Federal Military Archives

RHD 4, 138/12

RH 49/49

RH 53-7/v. 724

State Archives Munich

Staatsanwaltschaft Nr. 20988

Moosburg Municipal Archives

06/30

06/31

06/36

06/37

06/39

06/40

06/41

06/42

06/45

06/46

06/47

06/48

06/49

06/52

06/55

06/57

06/58

06/59

06/65

06/66

06/67

06/68

06/69

07/72

Bestand Stalag VII A Berichte Beginn-Ende

Bestand Stalag VII A Kulturelles Leben im Stalag

Stalag VII A Bildchronik Bd. II

Private Archive Karl A. Bauer

2. Printed sources

Files of the Party Chancellery, quoted from **Pfahlmann H.,** Fremdarbeiter und Kriegsgefangene in der deutschen Kriegswirtschaft 1939-1945, Darmstadt 1968, S. 187

Alckens A., Ein Tagebuch (29. April-22. Mai 1945), in: Keller M. (Hg.), Was ist geschehn?, Moosburg 1995, S. 87-129

Bericht des Stadtpfarrers Alois Schiml, in: **Pfister P.** (Hg.), Das Ende des Zweiten Weltkriegs im Erzbistum München und Freising, Teil II, München 2005, S. 842-848

Boberach H. (Hg.), Meldungen aus dem Reich, Herrsching 1984

Dtv (Hg.), Die Wehrmachtsberichte, 3 Bände, München 1985

Keller M. (Hg.), Was ist geschehn?, Moosburg 1995

Merkblatt „Verhalten gegenüber Kriegsgefangenen", herausgegeben vom OKW und dem Reichspropagandaministerium im Mai 1943, abgedruckt bei Pfahlmann H., Fremdarbeiter und Kriegsgefangene in der deutschen Kriegswirtschaft 1939-1945, Darmstadt 1968, S. 189

Merkblatt „Verhalten gegenüber Kriegsgefangenen", abgedruckt bei Pfahlmann H., Fremdarbeiter und Kriegsgefangene in der deutschen Kriegswirtschaft, Darmstadt 1968, S. 188

Schramm, P.E. (Hg.), Kriegstagebuch des Oberkommandos der Wehrmacht, Bd IV 2. Halbband, Frankfurt 1961

Sekretariat des Internationalen Militärgerichtshofs (Hg.), Der Prozess gegen die Hauptkriegsverbrecher vor dem Internationalen Militärgerichtshof, Nürnberg 1949, Bd. XXXVIII, S. 419-489

Stichpunktartiger Bericht des Domvikars Friedrich Frei, in: **Pfister P.** (Hg.), Das Ende des Zweiten Weltkriegs im Erzbistum München und Freising Teil I, München 2005

Weh L., Stalag VII A – Alpdruck und Schicksal der Stadt Moosburg in: Keller M. (Hg.), Was ist geschehn?, Moosburg 1995, S. 130-152.

Ziegler A., Ein Werk des Friedens, München 1979

II. Literatur

Albrecht D./Gelberg K. (Hgg.), Das Neue Bayern – Handbuch der Bayerischen Geschichte begründet von Max Spindler, Bd. IV 1. Teilband, München 2003, S. 635ff.

Bedürftig F., Drittes Reich und Zweiter Weltkrieg, München 2004, „Polenfeldzug"

Brückner J., Kriegsende in Bayern 1945, Freiburg 1987

Bullock A., Hitler, Düsseldorf 1961

Bullock A., Hitler und Stalin – Parallele Leben, München 1998

Churchill S., Der Zweite Weltkrieg, Bern 1985

Diem V., Die Freiheitsaktion Bayern, Kallmünz 2013

Fest J., Der Untergang, Hamburg 2003

Henke K., Die amerikanische Besetzung Deutschlands, München 1995

Keller R., Das deutsch-russische Forschungsprojekt „Sowjetische Kriegsgefangene" in: Bischof G./Karner S./Stelzl-Marx B. (Hgg.), Kriegsgefangene des Zweiten Weltkriegs, Wien 2005, S. 460-475

Keller R., Sowjetische Kriegsgefangene im Deutschen Reich 1941/42, Göttingen 2011

Mattiello G., Prisoners of War in Germany 1939-1945, Lodi 2003.

Mojonny G., The labor of prisoners of war in Modern Times, Locarno 1955

Mommsen H., In deutscher Hand – Der Arbeitseinsatz sowjetischer Kriegsgefangener 1941-1943 in: Haus der Geschichte der Bundesrepublik Deutschland (Hg.), Kriegsgefangene, Düsseldorf 1995, S. 141-147

Nowak E., Polnische Kriegsgefangene im Dritten Reich, in: Bischof G./Karner S./Stelzl-Marx B. (Hgg.), Kriegsgefangene des Zweiten Weltkriegs, Wien 2005, S. 507-517

Otto R., Wehrmacht, Gestapo und sowjetische Gefangene im deutschen Reichsgebiet 1941/42, München 1998

Pfahlmann H., Fremdarbeiter und Kriegsgefangene in der deutschen Kriegswirtschaft 1939-1945, Darmstadt 1968

Zwischen Vernichtung und Widerstand – Das Leben sowjetischer Kriegsgefangener im Stalag VII A Moosburg in: **Reither D./Rausch K./Abstiens E./Fößmeier C.,** Auf den Spuren verlorener Identitäten, Moosburg 2018

Speckner H., In der Gewalt des Feindes, Wien 2003

Spoerer M., Zwangsarbeit unter dem Hakenkreuz, München 2001

Streim A., Sowjetische Gefangene in Hitlers Vernichtungskrieg, Heidelberg 1982

Streit C., Keine Kameraden, Bonn 2001

Ziegler W., Bayern im Übergang. Vom Kriegsende zur Besatzung 1945, in: Pfister P. (Hg.), Das Ende des Zweiten Weltkriegs im Erzbistum München und Freising Teil I, München 2005, S. 33-104

The **author,** historian Dominik Reither, has also published among others the following books on Moosburg's history during the Second World War and its aftermath:

Stalag VII A Moosburg – Ein Kriegsgefangenenlager 1939-1945, Moosburg 2015 – ISBN 978-3743117983

Gemeinsam mit Karl Rausch, Elke Abstiens und Christine Fößmeier, M.A.:
Auf den Spuren verlorener Identitäten
– Sowjetische Kriegsgefangene im Stalag VII A, Moosburg/Norderstedt 2018 – ISBN 978-3746096087

Zwischen Hakenkreuz und Sternenbanner
– Kriegsende und Nachkriegszeit in Moosburg, Moosburg/Norderstedt 2020 – ISBN 978-3752699098

Internment Camp No 6 Moosburg
– Ein Internierungslager in der US-Zone 1945–1948, Moosburg/Norderstedt 2021 – ISBN: 978-3753482316

Unter Verdacht
– Im Internierungslager Nr. 6 Moosburg 1945-1948 Moosburg/Norderstedt 2022 – ISBN: 978-3756815814

Editor

The association **Stalag Moosburg e.V.** aims at researching and documenting the history of the prisoner of war camp Stalag VII A in Moosburg / Isar and its subsequent developments. International and intercultural encounters with citizens, visitors and relatives of former prisoners of war, events and projects shall help to preserve the historical heritage of the town in a way that is appropriate for the present and the future.

A comprehensive source of information about the Stalag VII A is provided by the website **www.stalag-moosburg.de**